Contents

KU-529-955

Note

THE edition of *Les Femmes savantes* referred to is the richly documented one by Gaston Hall, published by Oxford University Press in 1974. This edition reproduces the text of the original edition, but with modernized orthography, and with the minimum adjustment to the original punctuation. References in my text are to the line numbering, and, where appropriate, to act and scene numbers in the form of III, 4 (for Act III, scene 4) etc. References to other Molière texts are to the *Œuvres complètes* (edited by Georges Couton), published by Gallimard, Paris, Bibl. de la Pléiade, 1971. I have modernized the orthography of all quotations from secondary literature. Notes which refer to secondary literature mentioned in the Bibliography are in the form: author's name, italicized numeral or numerals related to the number of the item(s) in the Bibliography, with specific volume and page numbers, where appropriate. Bibliographical details of other works referred to are given in full in the notes.

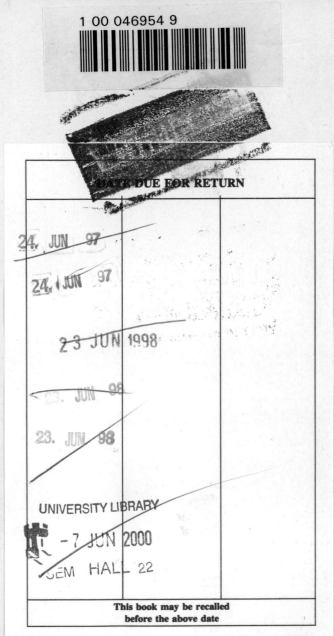

Critical Guides to French Texts

Critical Guides to French Texts

EDITED BY ROGER LITTLE, WOLFGANG VAN EMDEN,
DAVID WILLIAMS

MOLIÈRE

Les Femmes savantes

Noel Peacock

Senior Lecturer in French
University of Glasgow

Grant & Cutler Ltd
1990

© Grant & Cutler Ltd
1990

ISBN 0-7293-0314-4

I.S.B.N. 84-599-2931-0

DEPÓSITO LEGAL: V. 248 - 1990

Printed in Spain by
Artes Gráficas Soler, S. A., Valencia

for

GRANT & CUTLER LTD
55-57, GREAT MARLBOROUGH STREET, LONDON W1V 2AY

Introduction

L ES Femmes savantes, Molière's penultimate play, was
first performed on 11 March 1672 at the Palais-Royal.
Molière had taken out a *privilège* for the publication of the
play some fifteen months earlier (31 December 1670) to
protect himself against 'piratical publishers' and had regis-
tered the play on 31 March 1671. But it seems that the
comedy had been conceived as early as 1668:

> Le fameux Molière ne nous a point trompés dans l'espérance
> qu'il nous avait donnée il y a tantôt quatre ans de faire
> représenter au Palais-Royal une pièce comique de sa façon
> qui fût tout-à-fait achevée.[1]

The play has proved an enigma in the Molière canon. The
author himself seems to have considered it his most accomplished work, 'une pièce tout-à-fait achevée'. It was well
received in Molière's day: eight times the box-office receipts
topped 1000 *livres* and La Grange and Vivot in their edition
of Molière's works (1682) classified the play as one of
Molière's masterpieces along with *Tartuffe* and *Le Misanthrope.* But recent critical opinion has been less than enthusias-
tic: 'one of Molière's most savage plays' (*23,* p. 241); 'stale',
'muddled', 'misguided' (*42,* p. 356); 'sa plus mauvaise pièce,
et celui qui aime Molière ne l'y reconnaît plus qu'avec peine
[...] Cette œuvre trop soignée est sans verve' (*7,* III, p. 392).
The editor of the Pléiade edition of Molière's works is
disquieted by its 'âpreté', 'froideur' and lack of spontaneity (*2,*

---

[1] Donneau de Visé, *Le Mercure galant,* 12 mars 1672, p. 208. See *1,* vol.
IX, p. 3.

II, p. 975). Even Howarth, generally an admirer of the playwright, considers it a flawed masterpiece (*22* and *46*), and one of the most famous twentieth-century actors of Molière, Louis Jouvet, finds the play too dated to be comic (*24,* p. 62). The play contains some of the best known lines and scenes in Molière's work.

Yet it has been curiously neglected by producers outside the Comédie-Française (where it ranks fifth in popularity behind *Tartuffe, Le Médecin malgré lui, L'Avare* and *Le Misanthrope*). Neglect in the theatre may be explained on practical grounds: the play is primarily a 'pièce de troupe' and not a 'pièce d'acteurs' with eight roles longer than 100 lines, and therefore requiring eight accomplished actors. Another factor may be that the play stands on its own feet and does not lend itself to experimental productions in quite the same way as others. Producers cannot play about with the text or introduce gimmicks or transpose scenes – in that sense *Les Femmes savantes* is one of Molière's most sophisticated plays. A third possible explanation for its unpopularity, particularly in recent times, is its allegedly reactionary content.

Modern productions, following critical trends, have given a rather sombre rendering of the play.[2] Post-Freudian interpretations have turned Armande into the central figure and have transformed the *femme savante* into a *femme brûlante*. I shall attempt to reassess the play as a comedy and as a dramatic spectacle. The questions I seek to answer are fairly basic: what does the play do for us as spectators? how does the play work? what is the 'shape' of the play? These questions, however, are of fundamental importance, as the dramatist himself indicates in his preface to *L'Amour médecin:* 'les Comédies ne sont faites que pour être jouées'. I therefore propose to deal with matters of biographical or sociological import only as far as they illuminate Molière's aesthetic priorities. Historical aspects have tended to be discussed in isolation by critics. My method approaches that of W. G. Moore and R. Bray (*28* and *10*) who have set out

---

[2] See M. Descotes's review of productions by Jean Piat and Jean-Pierre Roussillon in 1978 (*Œuvres et critiques*, VI, 1 [1981], pp. 38-39).

general principles, but have not applied them in detail to *Les Femmes savantes*. My indebtedness to other critics is reflected in the notes and the Bibliography. I would, however, like to record my gratitude to Professor H. T. Barnwell for his invaluable suggestions and encouragement, and to the editors, Professors D. Williams and W. van Emden for their very helpful comments and advice.

1

Dramatic Effectiveness

LITTLE interest has been shown in the plot of *Les Femmes savantes*. Four reasons may be adduced for this: the unfavourable comparison of plot in comedy with that in tragedy; a tendency on the part of critics to view plot as secondary in Molière's dramaturgy to 'character development' and 'realistic observation', which, as Moore rightly objects (*28*, p. 68), are not the essentials of play-making; the fact that the basic plot of *Les Femmes savantes* is quite traditional – love rivalry and marriage against the will of one of the parties; and the seemingly static nature of Acts I, III and IV. I shall attempt to show the dramatic effectiveness of *Les Femmes savantes* by examining the means by which Molière manages to derive from a stereotyped motif suspense and tension – for the characters, if not always for the audience (for reasons which I shall examine in chapter 2).

In seventeenth-century dramatic theory much importance was attached to the exposition. With some of the audience sitting on the stage (in fact in what were regarded as the best seats), and no automatic control of lighting (the stage and the auditorium were lit by candle-power), a lively start was essential. Seventeenth-century engravings give evidence of the frequent interruptions of performances in which actors had failed to impose themselves favourably on the audience from the outset. The exposition of *Les Femmes savantes* has been dismissed as rather dull. The opening scene has been considered basically flawed, with the characters being supposedly vehicles for ideas in a *pièce à thèse* rather than human beings involved in a family conflict.[3] The colloquy between

[3] See W. V. Wortley, 'Molière's Henriette, an Imbalance between *Raison* and *Cœur*', *Romance Notes*, XIX (1978-79), p. 362.

the two sisters is not, however, dissimilar to the widely acclaimed first scene of other plays by Molière in which two brothers (*L'Ecole des maris*) or two friends (*L'Ecole des femmes, Le Misanthrope*) discuss rather heatedly general principles, then their particular application. In *Les Femmes savantes*, the theoretical discussion gives way to a personal one. The first half of the opening scene focuses on marriage and its *supposed* consequences (1-87), the second half (88-120) on the *actual* consequences. Molière introduces us immediately to the two worlds of the play, the collision between which will be a major source of tension – the world of self-styled intellect (Armande) and the world of self-styled matter (Henriette). The delayed explanation (in the second half of the scene) of the true reasons for the conflict takes us to one of the main problems of the play, the triangular love-plot: Henriette-Clitandre-Armande.

To convey the pre-existing situation to the audience, Molière works a variation on the *dépit amoureux* scene, a device frequently used to enliven earlier works (e.g. *Le Dépit amoureux,* IV, 3; *Les Fâcheux,* I, 5, II, 5) and reproduced in later plays (cf. *Tartuffe,* II, 4; *Le Bourgeois gentilhomme,* III, 8-10 [see *15,* pp. 82-96; *20,* pp. 3-18]). In most *dépit* scenes, the lovers' simulated disdain paradoxically reveals the genuineness of their affection. Molière inverts the process in *Les Femmes savantes* with Clitandre trying tactfully to convey to his former lover that he now loves her sister (I, 2).

Unlike the rapid exposition of many of Molière's comedies (which is sometimes contained in the first scene), that of *Les Femmes savantes* is deferred until II, 8. Future oscillations in the plot are signalled in I, 3 by three thumbnail sketches of characters yet to appear: Chrysale's kindly but weak disposition (205-08); Philaminte's authority in the household (209-14) and her cult of learning and veneration of Trissotin (227 ff.); Trissotin's pedantry and insipid poetry. The portraits are, however, coloured with dramatic irony: neither the lovers nor the audience are aware at this stage of the danger threatened by those portrayed. Philaminte's disclosure in II, 8 creates a new triangle: Trissotin-Henriette-Clitandre, which complicates the existing one and forms the central problem which has to be resolved. By protracting the exposition, Molière plays a guessing game with his audience, not dissimilar to the one Philaminte plays with Chrysale in II, 6. The exposition provokes comic suspense: we are kept wondering how much more is to come.

The dramatic interest is sustained during and after the exposition by Molière's interweaving of real and false obstacles to the lovers' happiness. In the first act, the real obstacle, Armande's spite and desire for revenge (I, 2) is presented before the false one, Bélise's romantic delusion that Clitandre is in love with her. In the second act, the pattern is reversed: Bélise's ludicrous intervention, which delays Ariste's attempt to brief Chrysale (II, 2-4), precedes the very real threat posed initially by the dismissal of the maid (II, 5), the character who traditionally supports the lovers in comedy, and confirmed by Chrysale's defeat in the battle for domestic supremacy and by Philaminte's disclosure (II, 6-8). From Act III onwards, with the arrival of the real adversary, Trissotin, the obstacles are no longer inconsequential: Philaminte's formal announcement of her intentions regarding Trissotin and Henriette (III, 4) and her bringing forward the wedding to that very evening (IV, 4). Attempts to remove the obstacles serve ironically to heighten the tension: Clitandre's second rejection of Armande (IV, 2) and attack on Trissotin (IV, 3-4) prove provocative; Chrysale's two unexpected appearances at the end of Acts III and IV only widen divisions within the household; Henriette's outburst in V, 1, however splendid, is fraught with danger; and Chrysale's final attempt to oppose his wife is undermined by his willingness to consent to a double marriage between Clitandre and Armande and Trissotin and Henriette (V, 3). Molière resolves the crisis by Ariste's artifice which comes as a *coup de théâtre* for the characters. This is the culmination of a series of unexpected twists in the plot; in particular, Philaminte's formal announcement of the wedding immediately after the initial humiliation of Trissotin in Act III, and her bringing forward the proposed wedding after his being further discredited in Act IV. As in most of Molière's plays, maximum dramatic potential is exploited by holding back the denouement until the very last minute.

Ariste's stratagem removes the chief obstacles to the marriage between Henriette and Clitandre – Trissotin's pursuit of Henriette for financial reasons and Philaminte's failure to recognize this and to perceive the generosity of Clitandre. With the dramatic problem resolved, Molière re-creates in the closing lines the comic suspense pervading the exposition by introducing two new complications based on false premises: Henriette's refusal of what she has worked hard to achieve throughout the play (1736 ff.) is made in ignorance of Ariste's artifice, and Bélise's objection (1774 ff.) is a fond figment of her imagination.

Another means by which the dramatic momentum is maintained is Molière's keeping apart for as long as possible characters who are in conflict with each other. Their eventual meeting is therefore made all the more climactic. The encounters between Philaminte and Chrysale, so crucial to the marriage interest, are restricted to two acts. Molière delays Philaminte's first entry until Chrysale has reached the point of supreme confidence, thus making the climb-down all the more dramatic. The repeat performance in V, 3 – this time in front of the Notaire – is brought about by Molière's use of intermediaries to relay messages between the two camps in Acts III and IV: Armande is ordered to convey to Philaminte details of Chrysale's latest pact (III, 6), while Clitandre passes on to Chrysale Philaminte's proposals (IV, 5). The similar containment within Acts II and V of the clashes between Martine on the one hand and Philaminte and Bélise on the other intensifies the central power struggle. These clashes act as a barometer of the domestic atmosphere and a pointer to the lovers' fortunes. The fate of the maid and that of the lovers have become inextricably linked to the conflict between husband and wife. The affirmation of Martine's unsuitability as a cook precedes that of Trissotin's eligibility as a husband for Henriette. Chrysale's readiness to sacrifice his servant in II, 6 is a dramatic portent of his sacrifice of his daughter in II, 8. His reinstatement of the maid in V, 2 shows his fresh resolve to reverse his wife's decision with regard to both Martine and Henriette. The two interviews between the former lovers, Clitandre and

Armande, are made all the more dramatic by their being separated by two acts and by the fact that the possible marriage between them is not ruled out until the very end of the play. The thinly veiled hostility in the presence of a third party (Henriette in I, 2 and Philaminte in IV, 2) contrasts sharply with the accord of Henriette and Clitandre in their only scene together in I, 3. The postponement of the show-down between the two rivals for the hand of Henriette marks the high point in a series of confrontations in Act IV, an act which has wrongly been dismissed as 'dramatically thin'. Molière orchestrates the conflict to a crescendo of abuse, terminated only by the arrival of Julien, whose message paradoxically revives another quarrel, that between Trissotin and Vadius. The holding back until V, 1 of the first tête-à-tête between Henriette and her would-be husband, Trissotin, sets a brisk tempo for the final act. The dramatic progression from Acts I to V is seen in the contrast between the lovers' somewhat composed review of obstacles (I, 3) and the desperate measures adopted by Henriette to dissuade Trissotin from going through with the marriage (V, 1). The rivalry between the sisters, which gives the play its initial dynamic, recurs at significant stages – overtly in III, 5-6 and covertly in the denouement. Such conflicts are augmented by unexpected confrontations between characters on the same side: Ariste and Chrysale (II, 9); Philaminte and Bélise (III, 2); Trissotin and Vadius (III, 3).

Far from being dramatically defective, *Les Femmes savantes* contains a greater number of conflictual situations and *coups de théâtre* than many of Molière's comedies. A play full of suspense and surprise is, however, not necessarily comic; in fact, in most cases it is not (see *21*, pp. 1-21). The comic depends on one's perspective and point of view, on the angle of perception. One of the functions of the dramatic is to provide the spectator with that perspective. The means by which this is achieved will be examined in the next chapter.

2

Comic Structure

M A N Y widely differing explanations of the comic have
been advanced by theorists from Plato to the present day.
Paradoxically, most of the treatises are dull and fail to reflect
the mode under consideration. Whereas one should not
underestimate the importance of theoretical writing for
seventeenth-century tragedy (cf. Corneille's *Discours* and
Examens and Racine's *Préfaces*), any attempt to prove that
Molière wrote his plays in strict conformity to discourses on
comedy would prove sterile. In any case, as an actor/play-
wright whose work was frequently commissioned at short
notice, Molière would have had little time for such an
exercise. Nevertheless, to try to explain comic aspects of
structure and of language, I shall relate the play to two
theories of comedy which have proved influential in Molière
studies but which have not been applied to *Les Femmes
savantes.* Bergson's treatment of the mechanical aspects of
laughter (see *9*) provide me with two headings, the use of
inversion and of repetition. However, my analysis of the
comic is largely derived from a theory of comedy published
four years before the appearance of *Les Femmes savantes,* an
anonymous publication entitled *La Lettre sur L'Imposteur*
(see *1*, IV, pp. 531-66), to which Molière may have contribut-
ed. It proposes two major principles: 'disconvenance' and
'excès'. The notion of 'disconvenance' (incongruity) posits
relativity and comparison:

> tout mensonge, déguisement, fourberie, dissimulation, toute
> apparence différente du fond, enfin toute contrariété entre
> actions qui procèdent d'un même principe, est essentiellement
> ridicule. (*1*, IV, p. 564)

There is nothing intrinsically comic about lying, disguise, trickery, deception, the four types of 'contrariété' cited above. Comedy arises solely from our intellectual perception of the contrast or discrepancy between two (or more) attitudes or actions. The contrast is not only, as Moore has suggested (*28*), between what is normative and what is unreasonable, but sometimes between two unreasonable elements.

The second principle in *La Lettre*, 'excès' (exaggeration), conveys a sense of unreality and even fantasy and appeals to the ludic instinct in us. We laugh at the cartoon figure because he is larger than life: harmful social ills have been neutralized by distortion. It is particularly in the realm of language that we shall discover this principle at work.

The appeal in comedy is primarily to the intellect or to the imagination rather than to the emotions. It presupposes what Bergson has referred to as an anaesthetizing of the feelings. The notional distance between audience and character, which is bridged in tragedy, is necessary for the comic principle to be effective. The audience views the comic spectacle with a feeling of intellectual and moral superiority and detachment.

Before examining the structure in the light of the comic principles I have enunciated, I draw attention to a common misapprehension: the equation of the comic with the laughable has led many to dismiss *Les Femmes savantes* as one of Molière's least successful works. The comic includes what is perceived retroactively as well as what is apprehended immediately; it embraces smile as well as the euphoria of farce.

ENTRANCES AND EXITS

I apply the principles of comedy to a subject rarely mentioned, but which forms an integral part of the comic spectacle. I shall consider firstly entrances which are untimely – from the entrant's point of view! Comedy depends on the superiority of the audience's knowledge to that of the characters. Clitandre is placed in a very delicate situation by Henriette in I, 2 when forced to choose publicly between the

two women he has courted (Molière here treats in a more
refined way the farcical scene between Dom Juan and the
peasants, with the main difference being that Clitandre does
love one of the women). The audience has been privy to
Armande's doubts about Clitandre's love for Henriette and
expectations of future conflict, aroused in I, 1, are almost
immediately fulfilled as Henriette's stratagem works against
the interests of the lovers. Trissotin also walks into a conflictual situation in IV, 3, just after a fourth unflattering portrait
of him has been supplied by Clitandre (1249-62). With
unconscious comic irony, Philaminte gives a cue to the actor
playing Trissotin:

> Si vous jugez de lui tout autrement que nous,
> C'est que nous le voyons par d'autres yeux que vous.
>
> (1263-64)

She puts him on the spot (1271-75) in using him as a weapon
against Clitandre. The pretext for Trissotin's return, his
announcement of an important scientific event, is doubly
ironic. At one level, the audience recognizes that the real
reason is the marriage interest. At another, it perceives the
incongruity between Trissotin's 'grande nouvelle' (the potential disintegration of the earth as a result of a close encounter
with the celestial world) and Philaminte's news (the marriage
between Henriette and the ethereal poet, which has provoked
the verbal collision of the previous scene). In III, 2, Henriette's inopportune arrival is comic in that she is unaware that
the poet she is compelled to listen to has been designated by
Philaminte as her future husband (II, 8). Vadius's entry in
III, 3 is just too late for him to hear the sonnet by Trissotin to
the *femmes savantes* in III, 2. In slating the work Vadius is
ignorant of its authorship, of the reception it has just been
given, and of the relationship which Trissotin has established
with the *femmes savantes*. In all these entrances, the audience
watches characters come on unsuspecting and stumble like
the victims in 'blind man's buff'.

The second type of comic entrance occurs when characters pop up either just when required or conversely when

least wanted. Chrysale appears just when Ariste wants to ask him to take up Henriette's cause (II, 2). Chrysale returns unexpectedly at the end of Acts III and IV, at the very moment that the lovers' cause seems beyond hope, and again in V, 2 after Henriette has lost her appeal against the marriage sentence to Trissotin (V, 1). The repetition of this type of entrance gives the impression of a puppet on a string. Molière's contrivance parodies the character's boast of freedom and authority.

Philaminte's entrance in Act II produces a volte-face on Chrysale's part, which is rendered the more comic by its repetition in Act V. His confident assertion: 'Et je ne veux pas, moi...' is cut dead by Philaminte's opening exclamation (428) and his bold affirmation: 'Nous verrons si ma femme, à mes désirs rebelle...' (1597) is instantly transformed into a plea for help at merely the anouncement of his wife's arrival. Ariste's entrances parallel and contrast with those of Chrysale. Chrysale's entrances do nothing to resolve the conflict whereas those of Ariste bring about the happy marriage. In II, 1 Ariste emerges to reassure the impatient Clitandre that all will be well, returns at the end of the act, and with his brother in Acts III and IV to promote the cause. The fact that Ariste does not accompany his brother in V, 2 makes the audience anticipate his entrance later in the act. The timeliness of his final appearance, which coincides with the moment of deepest distress for the lovers, emphasizes the difference between theatrical illusion (the reality of the play) and the reality of the audience. Bélise's entrances provide a comic pattern of interruptions. On her first appearance (I, 4) she takes Clitandre's request for help as a concealed proposal. The misunderstanding (*dialogue de sourds*) is prolonged despite Clitandre's protestations. On her second appearance (II, 3), the help she offers her brothers is taken at face value by the latter but ironically by the audience for whom the scene is a repeat performance of I, 4.

Another comic exploitation of entrances is seen in the way new characters fulfil or disappoint expectations aroused by portraits given of them prior to their arrival. Trissotin's delayed entry in III, 1 and performance in the sonnet scene confirm the three portraits sketched by Clitandre, Chrysale and Ariste in the first two acts: a fop and a simpleton whose writings are pretentious and devoid of substance (234, 251, 612); a foolish and boring pedant whose display of learning reveals his charlatanism (235-37; 689-91). The portraits of Vadius, on the other hand, are belied by the pedant's behaviour. The introduction by Lépine: 'Il est vêtu de noir et parle d'un ton doux' (928) and Trissotin's compliments: 'Il peut tenir son coin parmi les beaux esprits' (939)[4] take on ironical significance in the light of the slanging match in the second half of the scene.

Comic patterns are established between the various entrances and exits. The furtive entrances of Bélise (II, 3) and Clitandre (IV, 2) alert us to unexpected parallels between the two scenes. The discussions they overhear focus on Clitandre's courtship of Henriette. Neither eavesdropper is well-received: Clitandre's skilful attempts to dispel confusion and to defend himself make his critics more antagonistic, while Bélise's deluded efforts to enlighten her two brothers are for them a source of much mirth. The euphoric reception given to Vadius in III, 3 contrasts with that accorded his servant in IV, 4 which reflects the master's change in fortune and the superficiality of the *femmes savantes'* earlier enthusiasm. It prepares us for their disenchantment with Trissotin at the end of the play. The cordial greetings and nostalgic reminiscences of the distant past which give a relaxed atmosphere to the first meeting of the brothers in II, 2 contrasts with the hostility between the two sisters in I, 1, provoked by the evocation of the recent past, and with the imperious entry of Philaminte (II, 6), who comes on without greeting, and proceeds to discourse angrily on events which have taken place in the most recent past – the dismissal of Martine. Armande's tempestuous exits in I, 2 and III, 6 approach the maledictory tone of Vadius's departure (what a pity these two could not have come together!). Both characters go off to seek revenge,

---

[4] The image is drawn from the *jeu de paume*: 'un homme *tient bien son coin* quand il sait bien soutenir et renvoyer les coups qui viennent de son côté' (A. Furetière, *Dictionnaire universel,* The Hague, 1690).

but in order to gain it, Armande wants to promote the marriage between Henriette and Trissotin, while Vadius will do his utmost to block it. These instances of comic exits and entrances do not necessarily exhaust the subject, but they provide pointers for further exploration.

INVERSION

Perhaps the quintessential comic principle is that of inversion. By this, the dramatist is able to turn the world of the play upside down. The archetypal feature of the comic scene is the deceiver deceived, the situation which recoils on the head of the perpetrator of evil. The most obvious example of inversion is given in the denouement in which Trissotin is cheated by a device similar to the one he has used to cheat others. Yet most of the characters experience the comic degradation which such a reversal brings, albeit in more muted form. I shall analyse this comic principle firstly in the transition from confidence to anger brought about by the particular arrangement of the scene or of a group of scenes. Armande's confident assertions in I, 1 are deflated by the bi-partite structure of the scene and by the subsequent encounter with Clitandre. The assured tone in which she enjoins Henriette not to be vulgar (26-32), to become *savante* like their mother (37-42), to be wedded to philosophy, changes to a fit of pique as soon as the real motive for her counsel becomes apparent in the second half of the scene. Her anger increases in proportion to Henriette's ironizing. Henriette takes Armande's philosophical reasoning to its logical conclusion: that Armande is not interested in men, and therefore not in Clitandre. Ironically, Armande is defeated by the very weapons she has used against Henriette. On four occasions, Armande tries to evade the issue and change the direction of the conversation (109, 125, 155, 162). Each time Henriette is a match for her. Armande's last desperate measure, her appeal to the principle of parental choice (162-64) is turned back on her, as Henriette first asks Armande to help secure Philaminte's approval (I, 1), then, after Chrysale has publicly

confirmed his choice of Henriette for Clitandre (III, 6),
reminds Armande of her earlier stance. The situation is
repeated in Act IV. In the first scene she tries to turn her
mother against Clitandre, using tactics similar to those em-
ployed in I, 1. In the following scene, in her attempt to regain
him (1235-40), she renounces all the virtues of celibacy she
had extolled in the opening scene. Her deflation is aggravated
by Clitandre's rejection, which is all the more humiliating as
it is a repetition of his confession in I, 2. The third major
comic reversal for Armande is kept till the denouement in
which she reproaches the mother whom she has defended
throughout the play (1770).

The deflation of Bélise in II, 3 shows the affinity between
Bélise and her niece. Like Armande, though for different
reasons, Bélise sees herself as the object of Clitandre's affec-
tions. When Chrysale tries to disabuse her of her vagaries, she
flies into a rage and confirms the diagnosis of her brothers by
repeating the word 'chimères' six times (393-96).

Henriette is not discredited to the same extent. However,
her ability to provoke anger contributes to the total comic
effect. In I, 3, she gives advice in diplomacy to Clitandre –
somewhat ironic in view of her having put him in a very
difficult situation in the previous scene! Her attempts to
pacify him after his initial attack on Trissotin (230-36) serve
only to make Clitandre more irate (245-60). Her scepticism
with regard to her father's ability to honour his pledge (V, 2)
annoys Chrysale and threatens her support. After her first
speech in this scene, Henriette does not get more than a
hemistich in edgeways until 1595 and is reduced to half-
despairing, half-laughing agreement. Her failure to bolster her
father follows her failure to get through to Trissotin in the
previous scene. While the evolution of V, 1 is primarily a
commentary on the thickness of Trissotin's hide, it also
shows Henriette momentarily losing her temper. At one level
she exposes Trissotin for the fake that he is. His gallantry and
precious terminology are punctured by the crude and cynical
affirmation which Henriette's verbal dexterity forces him to
make: 'Pourvu que je vous aie, il n'importe comment' (1536).
At another level she experiences the same embarrassment as

her sister in I, 1. Henriette's conventional compliments and ironic self-denigration descend eventually to crude threats about the dangers of cuckoldry, which Trissotin is too insensitive (or too hypocritical) to take to heart. Henriette's futile adoption of some of her sister's tactics (Armande's *préciosité* and attempts to make her interlocutor afraid of the future) gives an ironic dimension to what is otherwise a bold and spirited venture.

Comic degradation is expressed in its most extreme form in the clash between Trissotin and Vadius in III, 3. The comic reversal is highlighted by the dramatic movement of the scene. In the first part, Vadius and Trissotin praise each other's works in fulsome style. Their reciprocal eulogies gather momentum and rise to a crescendo of flattery in which cause and effect become largely disproportionate. The turning point is Trissotin's request for Vadius's opinion of his poem (988). Vadius's peremptory judgement sets the precipitous forward motion in reverse: mutual compliments turn to alternating insults which are made more barbed by the use of *tutoiement,* appreciations of literary worth are replaced by accusations of plagiarism, and the scene ends with a challenge to a literary duel at Barbin's the booksellers. Further deflation is caused by the contradiction between theory and practice. Vadius condemns writers who continually bore their audience with their tiresome offerings and commends the example of a Greek who expressly forbade authors to launch into a public reading of their works. In his repeated attempts to read his ballad Vadius is guilty of the folly he censures in others. Molière's juxtaposition of Vadius's proscription and failure to heed it enhances the comic effect (963-68).

Comic irony underpins the scene. Both Trissotin and Vadius attack what they have not read. In addition, their praise is motivated by self-interest. On Vadius's part, it is an attempt to predispose Trissotin to listen to his ballad. Trissotin's flattery is calculated – paradoxically – to prevent Vadius from reading his work. Both tactics fail. Trissotin's first interruption (969) has the opposite effect to the one intended. His accolade makes Vadius all the more eager to offer his piece in the salon. When the pedant clears his throat in a second attempt to read his work (987-88) Trissotin's reference to his own poem precipitates the verbal combat. Vadius, for his part, is not subtle enough to disguise his self-interest and has not sufficient time or in fact the desire to enter into the inclinations of his listeners. His efforts to extricate himself from the embarrassing situation in which his unguarded remarks have placed him prove equally futile (1001, 1003-05). The egos of the two authors are further deflated by Vadius's letter in IV, 4. Trissotin's claim to originality in III, 2 is shown to be false in the light of his borrowings from ancient poets (Horace, Virgil, Terence, and Catullus). But Vadius's latest stratagem reveals his own hypocrisy, for he must have known about Trissotin's plagiarism when praising his work without qualification.

Act III scene 3 is also an ironic commentary on III, 2. Vadius's abortive attempt to read his work mirrors Trissotin's difficulties in the face of the repeated interruptions from Bélise, who provides a comic anticipation of the Greek scholar (756-58, 761, 765 ff.). The fact that Trissotin is able to read his sonnet is due less to his tactical skill than to the captive nature of his audience. The structure of III, 2, which also falls into two parts, prefigures that of III, 3. The reading of the sonnet and the epigram (756-841) releases a chorus of ecstatic cries from the bluestockings who vie with one another to discover the finest qualities in Trissotin's work. Their competitive spirit foreshadows Trissotin's and Vadius's attempts to outdo each other in compliments. The ladies never descend to the two men's level of abuse, but internal divisions are apparent in Philaminte's increasing anger over Bélise's interventions. The ladies' enthusiasm for inferior material matches the vacuous praise of Trissotin and Vadius. A comic reversal of roles is produced in the second half of III, 2 with the *femmes savantes* showing off their projects and Trissotin making approving noises. Had Trissotin maintained this ingratiating tone the quarrel with Vadius would not have taken place. But, by the same token, Vadius would have read his ballad and Trissotin would have lost his sole claim to the undiscerning admiration of the female pedants.

The quarrel between Vadius and Trissotin degrades the *femmes savantes* and reveals the extent to which they have become absorbed in their fantasy world. Trissotin's loss of status and dignity paradoxically strengthens Philaminte's faith in him, as she formally anounces the wedding in III, 4 and advances the date following Vadius's admonition in IV, 4. The *femmes savantes* are also deflated in Act III by two items of stage business. Lépine's fall (III, 2) sends up their over-elaborate preparations for the reading party. His inability to counter the effects of stumbling implies a physical inelasticity which mirrors the *femmes savantes*' linguistic automatism, which I shall analyse in the next chapter. Henriette's refusal to conform to the ladies' expectations reinforces the parody. Twice she attempts to leave the gathering and she dissociates herself from the hysterical welcoming of Vadius: 'Excusez-moi, monsieur, je n'entends pas le grec' (947).

The process of inversion in the dispute between Trissotin and Clitandre is more subtle (IV, 3). At first both men content themselves with vague affirmations (1281-92); the remarks become more wounding but the aspersions are still veiled (1293-1324) – Trissotin has learned more control after the débâcle with Vadius; but the criticism becomes more and more personal after Trissotin mentions the Court and impugns Clitandre as a courtier (1325-82). The temperature rises almost to the point at which the confrontation between Trissotin and Vadius had ended and is only lowered by the unexpected arrival of Vadius's messenger. Ironically, the message he brings will pour further scorn on the poet. As in III, 3 the pretensions of both Trissotin and the *femmes savantes* are mocked by the quarrel. Trissotin's conversation moves from the celestial (the shooting star) to the material ('les dons de la Cour' and his complaint about 'pensions'). The *femmes savantes* are powerless to influence the action. In III, 3, Philaminte's attempt to bring about a reconciliation was brushed aside (1018). In IV, 3 neither she nor Armande are able at first to complete a sentence (1313, 1317-18). In Philaminte's first uninterrupted remark, she tries to restrict the argument to generalities, to a kind of amorphous literary debate. Her exhortation is ironic in view of the results of the last symposium in III, 3 and of her next rejoinder – a personal attack on Clitandre (1385).

So far, my analysis has focused mainly on examples of the transition from confidence to anger. In the encounters between Chrysale and Philaminte we sometimes witness the reverse process: from anger to calm. This gives an ironic dimension to the traditional pattern of inversion in the play. Chrysale's celebrated outburst in II, 7 is too carefully orchestrated to be taken seriously. His anger is also muted after Philaminte's abrupt interjection: 'Comment donc?' by his pretending to address his remarks to Bélise – twice he turns to her to emphasize the point (558, 607-08) – and by his toning down criticism of what he considers to be the main source of his problem, namely his wife. In the next scene his anger gives way to docility. The comic reversal is threefold: Chrysale approves what he has condemned in II, 7 (Philaminte's upbringing of Armande, 625-26) as he tries to appease his wife; he acquiesces in Philaminte's proposal as a husband for Henriette of the very poet he has just been decrying (610-14); and he betrays the confidence he had shown in front of Ariste in II, 4. The reversal of roles between husband and wife, which is repeated in Act V, is amplified by the traditional reversal between master and servant. Philaminte's anger in II, 6 is at one level more productive than Chrysale's in that it achieves its end – the domination of Chrysale and in this instance the dismissal of Martine. But a comic let-down is produced by the disproportion between her excessive indignation and its trivial source, and the inversion of cause and effect and the delayed disclosure of the offence.

REPETITION

In my treatment of both entrances and exits and of the principle of inversion, the use of repetition has emerged as an important comic device. The repetition of conflicts (outlined in chapter 1) divorces the play from everyday reality and maintains the perspective of comedy. The central conflict between two opposing forces can be compared to what Bergson has described as a Jack-in-the-box toy. The Jack always manages to pop out, only to be pushed back again. The procedure is all the more comic if repeated and shown to be mechanical and automatic: the spring is bent, released, and bent again.

The repetition gives a pendulum-type motion to the play which serves a dual function. At one level it develops the original dilemma of the plot – the obstructions, barriers and obstacles to the lovers. At another it fulfils the expectation of comedy in conditioning our reflexes to react in a certain way so that we anticipate the outcome before the characters.

3

Comic Language

B Y far the greatest number of comic effects are produced on
the verbal plane. Yet, curiously, little attention has been paid
to this aspect of the play.[5] Many scholars are critical of
Molière for what they regard as a somewhat stilted style, and
postulate that one of Molière's friends, the poet Boileau, had
a hand in the play, creating plodding rhythms and pompous
diction. I shall examine the verbal means by which Molière
creates comedy: the language used by all the characters,
versification, and the significance of names in the play. The
language of the characters is revelatory of foibles, blind-
nesses and obsessions, which are expressed in forms of action
(the episodes and encounters I have considered in the previous two chapters). I shall analyse the lexis and syntax of the
characters not in isolation but in the different groupings
formed in the development of the plot.

THE *FEMMES SAVANTES*

Language is given a unique role by the *femmes savantes*.
It is their principal means of establishing a new society which
will replace the old order represented by Chrysale and his
supporters. For all three women language acquires the status
of a religion. The new order is founded on both prescription
and proscription. The god to whom all, including the cooks,
must pay homage is Vaugelas, a French grammarian
(1585-1650) whose *magnum opus* was published in 1647,

---

[5] Very interesting studies have focused on dramatic aspects of language:
G. Conesa, *13*; R. Garapon, *17*; E. J. Gossen, Jr, *41*; J. Molino, *48*.

entitled *Remarques sur la langue française.* Their brave
new world will be entirely spiritual, a world of words as
opposed to Chrysale's world of things. The ladies do not
consider cultivation of the 'bel usage' sufficient in itself.
Their linguistic doctrine contains an index of banned words
and constructions which they consider devoid of beauty (cf.
899-908). Hence their numerous criticisms of the language of
others (cf. 4-5, 10-11, 461, 487, 515 ff., 535, 615, 1601-02,
1612, 1699-1700).

Comedy is provoked by four things: the ladies' loss of
perspective, the inappropriateness of language to situation,
their violation of their own linguistic norms, and the self-
interested motivation for their linguistic reforms. The loss of
perspective, referred to in *La Lettre* as 'excès', is the hallmark
of all Molière's comic heroes. It reveals their obsessiveness, in
this case with learning or rather what passes for learning.
Linguistic purism is taken to extremes, even to the banning of
the 'syllabes sales' (909-14). They go further than the *précieuses* who wanted merely to proscribe words like 'car',
'encore', 'néanmoins', 'pourquoi'. Characters in the play are
categorized by the ladies according to the extent to which
they conform to or deviate from the prescribed code. Trissotin and Vadius are placed at the top of the new hierarchy
(immediately below the ladies), Chrysale and Martine at the
bottom. Chrysale is despised by Philaminte for his linguistic
earthiness ('Quelle bassesse, ô ciel, et d'âme, et de langage!'
[615]) and by Bélise for speaking like a bourgeois (616-17) –
which he happens to be! Martine is regarded as a criminal
(468) and is dismissed for a grammatical lapse – a punishment
grossly disproportionate to the offence. On the other hand,
Trissotin is admired as a practitioner of the purest aesthetic
form – poetry. Vadius is venerated as a specialist in Greek,
which represents, for the ladies, the most difficult and the
most erudite language, the language of the gods. The fact that
both men are pseudo-scholars confirms the superficiality of
the ladies' judgement and calls into question their grandiose
schemes for the reform of the language.

The lack of perspective is also seen in the *femmes savantes'* misuse of *précieux* language (recalling that of Cathos and

Magdelon in *Les Précieuses ridicules*): superlatives (e.g. 766, 818, 837, 909, 911-12, 923, 924-26, 1173, 1211), affective adverbs and hyperbole (e.g. 535, 769-70, 774, 792, 834). In addition, the use of repetition conveys the mechanical nature of their language. The repetition is sometimes of adjectives of opprobrium like 'bas' and 'sauvage' (26, 461, 1601); sometimes of antitheses (see in particular: 'haut / bas', 'noble / grossier', 'sens / matière', 'raison / animalité', I, 1); sometimes of exclamations (e.g. 'O ciel!', 493, 615); sometimes of hyperboles ('à nulle autre pareille', 459, 715); sometimes of synonyms (281) or even of the same word (e.g. 'chimères' and 'grec', 393-96, 943 ff.). The most comic expression of the ladies' automatism is in the sonnet scene, where stylistic parallels reveal the comic mechanism. In III, 1, Philaminte gives the lead and is followed by Armande and Bélise. The pattern is repeated three times. In III, 2, Molière works variations on this theme: Armande-Bélise-Philaminte (745-46); Armande-Philaminte-Bélise (755-58); Bélise-Armande-Philaminte; Armande-Bélise-Philaminte (765-70); Armande-Bélise-Philaminte (772-74); Bélise-Armande-Philaminte (776-79) etc. The moments when the three chant in unison show their verbal rigidity in its most extreme form (806, 827).

The fact that there are three *imaginaires* amplifies the element of disproportion and allows for comic gradation in the literary judgements (from Bélise's absurd misapprehensions to Philaminte's attempt at analysis). In II, 6 Philaminte's censure of the maid is incommensurate with the offence (479-80). Bélise's gloss reduces the initial reproach to absurd proportions (480-84). Similarly, in V, 3, Philaminte's criticism of the Notaire's language, criticism which is in itself inappropriate in context, is unwittingly parodied by Bélise's commentary (1601-02, 1605-09). Bélise's juxtaposition of Greek monies with Roman dates adds to the caricature (see *6*, p. 203, note to 1607 – the Greek origin of 'mines' and 'talents' and the Latin calendar 'ides' and 'calendes'). In the following scene, when Philaminte shows a deeper preoccupation with the word 'criminel' than with the loss of her lawsuit, the existing disproportion is made more ridiculous by our recall of the corrections made to the lawyer's language in the previous scene.

The automatic responses of the *femmes savantes* give comic emphasis to their linguistic absolutism, to their inability to adapt language to the different situations in which they are placed. Their fixed belief in what they regard as the universal significance of language is another facet of their mental blindness. Words for them are given meaning by the decrees of a particular authority on language (or rather, as we shall see, by their interpretation of such decrees), without reference to the context or to the kind of person who is speaking. The ladies' failure to relate language to situation leads to comic conflicts with all their interlocutors except Trissotin (whose flattery of the ladies pre-empts any criticism).

In the case of Bélise, the same failure leads to a complete breakdown in communication. Her main authority is the type of *galant* literature written by La Calprenède, Gomberville, Honoré d'Urfé and Mlle de Scudéry. Bélise superimposes the fictional model on to the reality of the play – Clitandre's love for Henriette. She tries to perceive ambiguity in unequivocal statements, believing that all men, and particularly Clitandre, are in love with her. When Clitandre, in an attempt to dispel the confusion, repeatedly mentions Henriette, Bélise attributes his tactics to the artifice of gallant lovers who feel they must avow their love indirectly, in Clitandre's case 'sous le nom d'Henriette'. Bélise takes the *femmes savantes*' attempt to purify the language to a paradoxical extreme: non-verbal communication. She reproaches Clitandre for using words to express his love for her (278-80). In the presence of Chrysale and Ariste, she justifies the silence of her many so-called lovers as a mark of respect (381-84).

The comic spiritualization of language is also seen in the coterie's use of metaphor. The background against which we may judge the comic effect is the reflections of Bouhours, Lamy and Rapin, whose writings on rhetoric call for restraint, simplicity and naturalness (see *36*, p. 44, n. 1). The abusive use of figurative meanings can be seen in the clumsy abstraction of culinary imagery from its literal context. Bélise gives an absurd lead: 'Ce sont repas friands qu'on donne à mon oreille' (716). Philaminte extends the image: 'Servez-nous promptement votre aimable repas' (746), and Trissotin's elaboration loses all sense of proportion (747-54). Such figurative language is triply ironic: firstly, the *femmes savantes* do live off words; secondly, Trissotin's sonnet would hardly sustain anyone; and thirdly, the culinary images contrast with Chrysale's alimentary terms: 'Je vis de bonne soupe, et non de beau langage' (531).

The inappropriateness of language to situation, the second principle under consideration, but one which overlaps with the first, illustrates the *femmes savantes'* lack of judgement. In the sonnet scene, we are given an excellent demonstration of how not to do an *explication de texte*: paraphrase, verbatim quotations, ecstatic repetition (and swooning), empty exclamation, culminating in the most unanalytical interjections: 'Oh, oh' (787) and 'Ah!' (804, 805, 827). The popular 'caquets' (789) and the onomatopoeically evocative 'Quoi qu'on die' suggests (amongst other things!) the farmyard rather than the literary salon. After the reading of the sonnet, their enthusiasm for philosophy is expressed in a welter of equally uncritical terminology. As Hubert has remarked, Armande's 'Epicure me plaît', Philaminte's 'Pour les abstractions j'aime le platonisme', and Bélise's 'Je m'accommode assez pour moi des petits corps' are more appropriate to the selection of a new dress or to the latest craze in lace (*23*, pp. 244-45). Ironically, when critical terminology is used, it is misdirected. Bélise gives a grammar lesson to the maid in a language which the latter finds incomprehensible and a physics lesson on gravity to Lépine, when the servant, who has just fallen to the ground, is in no position to appreciate its worth! (Note the comic contrast between painful *experience* and inappropriate *theorizing*.)

Heroic vocabulary is also misused (*23*, p. 243). Philaminte conjures up an epic struggle with words like 'souveraine', 'pouvoir', 'empire', 'loi', to depict the hen-pecking of Chrysale. Armande sounds like a young emperor planning a *coup d'état:* 'nous y prétendons faire des remuements [...] Contre eux [les mots] nous préparons de mortelles sentences' (900, 905). Her high moral tone elsewhere, which has been equated with Rodrigue's ethical stance in *Le Cid,* is rather melodramatic in the non-political and non-military context of *Les Femmes savantes* (see *6,* p. 199, note to 1174). Armande's tragic diction at the end of the play has led critics to view her as 'le grand douloureux de la pièce', 'une martyre crucifiée', and to compare her with Eriphile, one of Racine's most unfortunate heroines in *Iphigénie,* or with the decadent and neurotic characters in Ibsen or in Wagnerian opera. Armande's closing line is, however, mock-heroic, and undermines the claims she makes to stoic control in earlier scenes (cf. 1145-48).

Bélise's misuse of religious terminology parallels Armande's and Philaminte's misuse of heroic language. Clitandre's supposed love for her takes on the proportions of a biblical allegory. The 'figure' (305) and the 'voile ingénieux' (367) are signs to the initiated just as the obscure passages in the Old Testament held significance only for those who 'had eyes to see and ears to hear'. Other inappropriate images emphasize the linguistic incompetence of the *femmes savantes.* On occasion Philaminte uses metaphorically expressions to which Chrysale gives a literal application: 'Que de science aussi les femmes sont meublées' (869) takes up Chrysale's 'Vous devriez brûler tout ce meuble inutile' (563). The juxtaposition of sewing imagery and terms of rhetoric (518-20) shows Philaminte's inability to escape from the domestic sphere and ironically anticipates Chrysale's prescribed occupation for women (583-84). Elsewhere Philaminte's equestrian image ('la main haute') clashes with two preceding expressions ('heurter le fondement' and 'régenter', 464-66). Her over-dramatized censure of Martine's solecism is rendered inappositely by 'En voilà pour tuer une oreille sensible'. Bélise's concrete imagery to describe a similar phenomenon ('Il est vrai que l'on sue à souffrir ses discours / Elle y met Vaugelas en pièces tous les jours', 521-22) seems to have been drawn from the area of the kitchen. Her fusion of technical and prosaic ('Un esprit composé d'atomes plus bourgeois', 617) and her self-cancelling, cacophonous 'ou le pléonasme ou la cacophonie' (524) are likewise ironic; Armande's popular expressions 'claquemurer', 'tousser et cracher comme elle', 'marmot' make us suspicious of her metaphors of gallant love in I, 1.

The linguistic aspirations of the *femmes savantes* are further belied by their violation of their own linguistic norms, the third feature under consideration. Philaminte has not read her Vaugelas with sufficient care! His definition of 'le bon usage' in his preface contradicts their disdain of the courtly Clitandre and of contemporary writing: 'la façon de parler de la plus saine partie de la Cour, conformément à la façon d'écrire de la plus saine partie des Auteurs du temps'.[6] Vaugelas attaches little weight to reason: 'L'usage fait beaucoup de choses par raison, beaucoup sans raison, et beaucoup contre raison',[7] whereas Philaminte's system is founded, she pretends, on 'la raison' and 'le bel usage' (475-76, 517). The fact that Philaminte's system is founded on neither reason nor Vaugelas gives double irony to her claim.

Philaminte also ignores Vaugelas's conception of the necessary correlation between mode of speech and milieu. The possibility of a maid speaking the language of the upper classes was never envisaged by the grammarian (though he admitted that his notes to his valet were as carefully written as anything else). Furthermore, Philaminte's objections to the barbarity of the legal terminology in which the marriage contract is drawn up (1601-02) is contradicted by the very Vaugelas whose authority she invokes: 'Le plus habile Notaire de Paris se rendrait ridicule et perdrait toute sa pratique, s'il se mettait dans l'esprit de changer son style et ses phrases, pour prendre celles de nos meilleurs Ecrivains' (see note 7, p. 144). Chrysale's reference to 'les lois de Vaugelas' (525) highlights the false impression of the grammarian conveyed by the bluestockings, who have ignored Vaugelas's unpedantic refusal of the title of legislator. (Vaugelas emphasized that he

---

[6] *Remarques sur la langue françoise* (Facsimile de l'édition originale), Paris, Droz, 1934, Section II.

[7] See *Les Femmes savantes,* ed. F. Spencer, London (The Temple Molière), 1907, pp. 130-31.

was only the minute-taker of a sort of court in which decisions were handed down by 'le bon usage'.)

The female pedants' abhorrence of archaisms is undermined by their own use of outmoded expressions. Philaminte borrows the archaic legal terminology ('assister à signer', 1407) to invite Clitandre to the proposed wedding between Henriette and Trissotin. Bélise's claim to dislike anything old-fashioned runs counter to her archaic lexis: 'vouer leur service', 'hors de page' (383, 862). It is ironic that in 'collet monté' (554) Bélise uses a term which had been out of vogue since 1630 (and perhaps since 1600) to support Philaminte's denunciation of Chrysale's obsolete expression.

The *femmes savantes'* fixation about grammatical accuracy is parodied by curious lapses in their own syntax. Having reproached Martine for breaking the laws of agreement between verb and subject, adjective and noun, Bélise perpetrates a similar error: 'Grammaire est prise à contresens par toi' (493) should, according to Auger, have read 'Grammaire est pris', as she is commenting on the use of the *word* grammar (cited in *1*, IX, p. 99, n. 3). In any case she is a fine one to criticize another for 'contresens', having cultivated ambiguity and misinterpreted plain speaking. Armande, too, fails to make an agreement – ironically, in formulating the ladies' unique claim to correct usage: 'Et ne verrons que nous qui sache bien écrire' (926). (At best the expression would be very elliptical with *qui* referring to *personne qui*.)

As for lexis, Bélise misuses the technical terms of grammar: the words 'nominatif' (497) and 'se décline' (838) may be applied only to languages which have inflected cases and noun endings. She also berates Martine for pleonasm and cacophony (524), failings which the audience perceives in Bélise's language (e.g. the six-fold repetition of 'chimères' (393-96), the redundant preposition in 'prendre le pas devant' (546) and the cacophonous repetition of 'quoi qu'on die'). Philaminte's insistence on precision is deflated by her vague: 'Je n'ai rien fait en vers' (844), a statement refuted by Armande in 1155-56. Philaminte means: 'Je n'ai point fait de vers depuis peu, depuis ceux que je vous ai lus' (*1*, IX, p. 132, n. 3).

Another comic contradiction of the ladies' linguistic principles lies in the involuntary sexual associations of many of their comments in III, 2, which vitiate their intention to purge all syllables which may be used for indecent jests:

> Ces sources d'un amas d'équivoques infâmes,
> Dont on vient faire insulte à la pudeur des femmes.
>
>   (917-18)

Philaminte invites us to scrutinize each word (712) and, paradoxically, to look for deeper meanings (790-92), and asks Trissotin if he has understood all the hidden depths (795-96). Bélise, too, thinks she perceives more than the literal interpretation (793).
Molière indulges in a game of metaphorical procreation. Trissotin compares his sonnet to the birth of a child of whom he is the father and Philaminte, the audience who receives it, the mother (720-24). The ladies' anticipation of and response to the reading is expressed in terms of a passionate love-affair. The prelude:

> Je brûle de les voir [...] Et l'on s'en meurt chez nous [...] Ce sont charmes pour moi, que ce qui part de vous [...] Ne faites point languir de si pressants désirs [...] Dépêchez [...] Faites tôt, et hâtez nos plaisirs.   (713-18)

The response to Trissotin's: 'Faites la sortir quoi qu'on die':

> Ah tout doux, laissez-moi, de grâce, respirer [...] Donnez-nous, s'il vous plaît, le loisir d'admirer [...] On se sent à ces vers, jusques au fond de l'âme / Couler je ne sais quoi qui fait que l'on se pâme.   (776-79)

And the climax, after the reading:

> On n'en peut plus? [...] On pâme [...] On se meurt de plaisir [...] De mille doux frissons vous vous sentez saisir [...] Partout on s'y promène avec ravissement.[8]   (810-11, 814)

---

[8] For a more detailed analysis of erotic elements in the poem and its reception see: J.-H. Périvier, *50* and Josette Rey-Debove, *51*.

This 'displaced sexuality' reveals an essential vulgarity which the *femmes savantes* seek to cover with a veil of prudishness, seen here, not least, in the incongruous use of the impersonal form 'on'. Armande's libidinous expressions in the sonnet scene debase retroactively her attempts in the first scene to dress up, by the use of abstraction and periphrasis, the physical realities of marriage: 'Le beau nom de fille [...] vulgaire dessein [...] un tel mot [...] aux suites de ce mot [...] de tels attachements [...]' (1, 4, 10, 14, 19). Furthermore, our recall of the uninhibited expressions of ecstasy in III, 2 makes us smile at the difficulties she faces when she throws herself at Clitandre in IV, 2 but refuses to pronounce the word marriage: 'des nœuds de chair, des chaînes corporelles [...] ce dont il s'agit' (1238, 1240).

The self-interested motivation of the *femmes savantes'* theories of language (my fourth consideration) betrays their affinity with Molière's other monomaniacs who see every issue from their own narrow and selfish point of view. The *femmes savantes* evolve their linguistic reforms to attain superiority. Their correction of the language of Henriette, Chrysale, Martine, and the Notaire is intended to give themselves power over these characters. The dismissal of Martine betrays the self-centred aspect of their pedantry. They are preoccupied as much with her failure to obey their lessons as with her infringement of Vaugelas's linguistic code:

Elle a, d'une insolence à nulle autre pareille,
Après trente leçons, insulté mon oreille [...]
Et des lois du langage on l'a cent fois instruite.

(459-60, 472)

The use of abstraction by Armande is designed to set her apart from ordinary humanity – a status she wishes to relinquish as the play progresses!

The *femmes savantes'* appreciation of Trissotin's poems is calculated to gain them distinction. Philaminte's desire for superiority is not restricted merely to domination of Chrysale and Henriette. She believes she has discerned qualities that no one else, not even the author, has perceived in the poem. Her vanity is also expressed in her eagerness to bring the conversation round to her own projects.

Like the doctors and lawyers in other plays by Molière, the ladies use jargon to impress others and to prove the extent of their knowledge (e.g. 'congrûment', 'récidive', 'négative', 'nominatif', 'substantif', 'd'oraison', 'pléonasme', 'cacophonie', 'épiderme' (482-85, 497-98, 518, 524, 1065). Their comic self-assertiveness is confirmed by other features of language, in the first place by the use of the imperative and the rhetorical question. In II, 6, Philaminte alternates between imperatives to the maid and rhetorical questions to her husband which take away the freedom of either to disagree with her. She follows this with a succession of exclamatory affirmations which she regards as unchallengeable. In Act V she addresses her husband in the imperative mood as she seeks to regain her control over him. Armande shows similar aggression in the opening scene as she tries to impose her will on Henriette. She fires a series of questions to which she does not expect an answer. The fact that she receives one from Henriette pricks the bubble of her superiority. When Armande's rhetorical questions fail, she resorts to simple imperatives (there are eight in one speech [26 ff.]) – but without any greater success. The predominance of imperatives and rhetorical questions in the language of Philaminte and Armande shows their virile determination and their desire to take over from men.

Bélise's use of the imperative (there are six in her opening speech) betokens the dotty school-mistress who feels a compulsion to indoctrinate everyone she meets on matters of gallantry or on elements of grammar. The tendency to interrupt their interlocutors (sometimes one another) manifests a lack of control, an unwillingness to listen to the point of view of others and their preoccupation with their own argument. The repeated juxtaposition of superlatives and possessive adjectives and pronouns to affirm that everything will be judged according to their rules ironically demonstrates to the audience the subjective nature of their belief in the universal significance of language:

> Nous serons par nos lois les juges des ouvrages.
> Par nos lois, prose et vers, tout nous sera soumis.
> Nul n'aura de l'esprit, hors nous et nos amis.
> Nous chercherons partout à trouver à redire,
> Et ne verrons que nous qui sache bien écrire.
>
> (922-26)

They imagine themselves capable of creating for themselves an exclusive and unrealizable élite: an aspect of their characteristics as *imaginaires*.

THE POETASTER AND THE PEDANT

The fact that their two models fare no better linguistically is a further ironic comment on the ladies' pretensions. Both Trissotin and Vadius reflect their hostesses' vanity and pomposity. Trissotin, in his self-congratulatory introduction to his poem (754), and in his name-dropping (751); Vadius, in his determination to read his poem (even in his letter he still pleads for an audience) and in his display of learning: note the affected expressions laced with mythological references (970) and with terms from Greek rhetoric (972) to reiterate Trissotin's eulogy of the previous line. Ironically, his Greek is as unintelligible to the *femmes savantes* as Bélise's technical terms were to Martine.

The ladies' loss of perspective is echoed by misappropriation of authorities in III, 3: Vadius's pastorals according to Trissotin surpass even those written by the greatest classical exponents of the genre, Virgil or Theocritus, while Trissotin's odes, for Vadius, leave Horace far behind. Philaminte's ludicrous claim to have superseded Plato (846-48) is, by the latest scale of comparison, fairly moderate!

Both Trissotin and Vadius fail to sustain the elevated tone. As we have seen in chapter 2, their sophisticated terminology is quickly reduced to fish-wife invective. In Trissotin's sonnet the lack of verbal inventiveness is seen in the clumsy rhyming of two adverbs ending in '-ment', in the forced elaboration of precious metaphors, which are also vitiated by the concrete ending: 'Noyez-la de vos propres mains'. The conclusion of the poem is also conceptually absurd: how can one 'noyer de ses propres mains' something which is inside one? (See *49*, p. 410.)

Trissotin's and Vadius's confused use of terms exposes the bluestockings' ignorance and also their own lack of grasp. Vadius's false attribution of a line from Horace's *Ars poetica* to a Greek author (964) may be a conscious appeal to the ladies' newly acquired enthusiasm for the ancient language. Trissotin's dedication of his poetry to the Corinthian courtesan 'Ma Laïs!' (832) is somewhat ambiguous in the context of sexual innuendo. The ladies' contempt for archaic forms is mirrored in Trissotin's criticism of the ballad ('La ballade, à mon goût, est une chose fade. / Ce n'en est plus la mode; elle sent son vieux temps', 1006-07). But just as the ladies' carping criticism of Chrysale is motivated by their desire to assert their superiority, so this objurgation is provoked by the reversal in the relationship between Trissotin and Vadius, rather than by any serious misgivings about the particular genre.

Trissotin's duplicity, like the affectation of the ladies, is confirmed by incongruities in his language. In his role of lover, he goes through the gamut of precious platitudes to win over Henriette. Yet even before his celebrated self-betrayal (1536), he lets slip his mercenary instincts:

> Votre grâce et votre air, sont les biens, les richesses,
> Qui vous ont attiré mes voeux et mes tendresses;
> C'est de ces seuls trésors que je suis amoureux.

> (1473-75)

After Trissotin's financial expressions in the sonnet 'riche appartement' (774), 'Qu'il m'en coûte la moitié de mon bien' (828), his complaint about the loss of 'pensions' in IV, 3, and Vadius's indictment of him as a fortune-hunter, we are made more attentive to the comic ambiguity of the poet's language.

THE CONSERVATIVES: CHRYSALE, MARTINE, ARISTE

The conservatives represent the material world of which the *femmes savantes* are so critical. They act as a foil or feed to the ladies and expose their ridiculousness. Concrete expressions and literal-mindedness contrast with abstraction and abstruse metaphorization. Chrysale's infernal imagery 'vrai dragon' (674), 'sa diablerie' (675) gives to the audience a comic focus on Philaminte's repeated homilies on the spiritual dimension of life (cf. 538). His list of material objects, 'rabats', 'pourpoints', 'soupe', parallels the ladies' catalogue of grammatical terms. The use of *bas langage* (especially the repetition of 'pot') sets off an automatic reaction in Philaminte (an actress playing the role at the Comédie-Française flinched repeatedly during Chrysale's famous tirade in II, 7). Chrysale's graduated enumeration of the possible reasons for the dismissal of Martine – breakage of a mirror or of a rare and valuable piece of pottery or theft – allows the audience to see the scale of Philaminte's folly. Not that Chrysale is incapable of abstraction. In fact, he uses it in II, 7 to make his attack more cutting (cf. 'Le raisonnement en bannit la raison').

Martine's unpretentious expression may likewise be interpreted as a conscious parody of the *femmes savantes*. Her verbal fantasy has been ignored until recently (see *17*, pp. 148-49). The question as to whether she is naive or mischievous is an open one. In either case, laughter is possible. It is, however, noticeable that she reserves her most extreme deformations of language for her encounters with the ladies: patois (478, 486) 'biaux' for 'beau', 'cheux' for 'chez' (Vaugelas mentions 'cheux' as one of two examples of bad pronunciation); popular expressions, 'se gourment' (503); misconstructions like the use of a double negative 'ne servent pas de rien' (478); popular improprieties: 'épiloguer' for 'ratiociner' (1657); words confused with their homonyms, 'grand'mère' for 'grammaire' (492) – *grammaire* was pronounced like *grand'mère* in the seventeenth century; solecisms: 'je n'avons pas étugué' (485), 'je sommes' (1641), 'je parlons' (486). Elsewhere she shows a capacity for a more refined diction: the use of the term 'cadrer' (1666) made one contemporary critic, Bussy Rabutin, question the coherence of the role. At other times, she uses the imperfect subjunctive and correctly manipulates imperfects and conditionals (1647-52). All of which makes me agree with Garapon that we laugh with Martine more than at her.

Her farmyard maxim: 'La poule ne doit pas chanter devant le coq' (1644) inverts the lofty proposition of Philaminte:

> Et qui doit gouverner ou sa mère, ou son père,
> Ou l'esprit, ou le corps; la forme, ou la matière.

(1129-30)

which itself inverts traditional Aristotelian terminology 'by which the man was considered to supply the form in procreation, the woman only matter'. Martine's implicit comparison between women and hens caricatures Armande's professed disdain for the 'partie animale / Dont l'appétit grossier aux bêtes nous ravale' (47-48), which Henriette had already parodied in more elevated language: 'Où donc est la morale / Qui sait si bien régir la partie animale, / Et retenir la bride aux efforts du courroux?' (159-61).

Ariste provides an ironic focus on the pedantic language of Trissotin ('six mots de latin') and his singularly inept poetry (690-94), and tries to bring his sister to an awareness of her fantasies (II, 3). He also attempts to goad his brother into activity, sometimes by an accumulation of synonyms denoting approbation: 'Fort bien', 'Il est vrai', 'Sans doute' (II, 9), at others by invective. However, none of the conservatives offers the linguistic norm of the play. Chrysale and Ariste have mistakenly been called *raisonneurs* (in fact, the term is a misnomer).[9] In all three roles there is a comic double edge or what *La Lettre* calls 'contradictory actions proceeding from the same source'.

---

[9] See my article: 'The Comic Role of the *Raisonneur* in Molière's Theatre', *MLR,* 76 (1981), pp. 298-310.

In Chrysale, the discrepancy between verbal posture and reality recalls that of the *femmes savantes*. His repeated expressions of authority are belied by each encounter with his wife. His confident assertions in front of Ariste and Martine: 'Il suffit, je l'accepte pour gendre [...] Il n'est pas nécessaire / Je réponds de ma femme et prends sur moi l'affaire [...] C'est une affaire faite [...] Et je ne veux pas, moi [...]' (II, 4-5), after Philaminte's arrival, fade into embarrassed, evasive, even monosyllabic utterances: 'Eh!', 'Mon Dieu, non', 'Je ne dis pas cela', 'Eh bien oui', 'D'accord', 'Aussi fais-je', 'Si fait', 'Je n'ai garde' (II, 6). He glosses over his weakness with euphemisms, referring in II, 9 to his pusillanimity in the previous scene as 'douceur' and 'facilité'. Verbs and nouns denoting volition, expressions of necessity, absolutes and imperatives trip off his tongue in Philaminte's absence as he attempts to bolster his ego and to demonstrate to his supporters his exclusive right to power (cf. 1564-66, 1586-94). His recourse to the imperative in her presence in V, 3 does not express any new initiative. He is merely parroting his wife. In this, he differs little from his sister. What comic potential Molière drew from the old adage: 'blood is thicker than water'! Chrysale cannot act, but merely verbalizes, and even then only when his opponent is not present.

He also evinces the lack of perspective of the coterie. He uses a military metaphor ('nous donnions chez') to describe his amorous conquests in Rome (345-49). But his escape into the dreams of youth (cf. Bélise), his servile attempts to keep his wife in good humour, and his willingness to hand over Clitandre to Armande in V, 3 show an obtuseness in matters of the heart, which contradicts his 'fredaines'.

Like Bélise, Chrysale fails to distinguish between illusion and reality in his sweeping generalizations about both genuine theoreticians of language and the bogus Trissotin (533-34): François Malherbe (1535-1628) was a celebrated purist and reformer of French poetry, who laid down rules for French prosody; Jean-Louis Guy de Balzac (1594-1655) was recognized for a carefully studied, formal style which enriched the French language. Chrysale's total disregard of form is as extreme as the *femmes savantes'* abusive attention to it.

The linguistic norm for Martine (illustrated by her aphorism: 'Quand on se fait entendre, on parle toujours bien', 477) paradoxically ignores the manner of expression and is subverted by the next line: 'Tous vos biaux discours ne servent pas de rien', an error which sets the *femmes savantes'* grammar machine in motion. Furthermore, Martine's words in Act V on the proper hierarchy of husband and wife are contradicted by the ironic situation she has placed herself in as the spokeswoman of Chrysale ('Ce n'est point à la femme à prescrire, et je sommes / Pour céder le dessus en toute chose aux hommes', [1641-42]).

Ariste's language is not elegant enough to be regarded as normative. His speech is replete with factual statements and prosaic utterances. He is full of good advice and encourages his brother to assert his will. But he does not have to address himself to Philaminte.

THE LOVERS

The linguistic norm of the play is provided by Clitandre and Henriette, two roles which have been dismissed as among the dullest in Molière's theatre and as almost a mistake on the author's part. Their conscious manipulation of language contrasts with the verbal rigidity of the pedants, particularly Armande and Trissotin. In I, 2, Clitandre performs a mini-drama with Armande as the heroine (he himself playing a subordinate role – a rare performance by a Molière character!). He uses abstract nouns, 'tendres soupirs', 'l'ardeur [...] désirs', to anticipate the reaction of Armande, to act as a buffer, to create a distance between himself and his interlocutor, to avoid giving offence (after all, he is still fond of her). His use of personification ('Mais vos yeux [...]', [140 ff.]), while conventional, is a way of toning down responsibility for remarks which are obviously unpalatable to Armande. In IV, 2 his real verbal elegance is again evident in his parrying the attacks of Armande and her mother. He takes 'the sting out of his remarks by making the subject abstract: "la fierté", and does not even attach it directly to Armande by a possessive adjective, let alone use the personal pronoun' (*36*, p. 46). Clitandre, who moves in Court circles, shows the *femmes savantes* how to use impersonal constructions and abstractions correctly. His recourse to precious terminology in IV, 3 makes his attack on Trissotin more pointed. Clitandre imitates Trissotin's love of paradox, paradoxically, to make fun of the aphorisms of the poet.

Henriette parodies her sister's elevated expressions in I, 1, at times by imitating them: 'élévations', 'spéculations', 'les hautes régions de la philosophie', 'les terrestres appas', 'les bassesses humaines'; at others, by ironically chosen bourgeois metaphors: 'fabriquer', 'étoffe', 'taillée'. Henriette maintains ironic detachment throughout the performances of Trissotin and Vadius in Act III. In V, 1 she resorts to the precious style of her interlocutor,[10] as Clitandre had done in IV, 3, though not to provoke Trissotin but rather to dispose him to her request. She turns the weapons of her adversaries against them: witness her recourse in 1488 to a precious expression used by her aunt in 619 to dissociate herself from Chrysale ('me vouloir mal de').

Despite their considerable verbal skill, the lovers are not immune to our laughter: Clitandre's insensitivity towards Henriette in explaining to Armande that he has only turned to Henriette in despair, 'le rebut d'autres charmes' (148); the archetypal earnestness of the lover as seen in Ariste's triplet of futures, presumably in response to three imperatives from Clitandre: 'J'appuierai, presserai, ferai tout ce qu'il faut. / Qu'un amant, pour un mot, a de choses à dire! / Et qu'impatiemment il veut ce qu'il désire!' (330-32); Clitandre's immoderate attack on the verbal flow of the pedants, which, paradoxically, furnishes Molière's theatre with one of its longest sentences (1363-82); and the occasional dropping of the polite mask: 'Je veux être pendu si je vous aime' (323). Henriette, too, occasionally miscalculates the appropriate language. In the final scene, she applies the stereotyped terminology of the romantic heroine to a curiously unroman-

---

[10] Cf. 'trouble', 'vœux', 'appas', 'feux généreux', 'amoureuse ardeur' (used twice), 'les hommages d'un cœur', 'l'éclat de sa gloire'.

tic situation: refusal of Clitandre on grounds of seeming financial straits.

The linguistic norm projected by the lovers is therefore a comic one. As we have seen in chapters 1 and 2, their stratagems do not advance their cause. The obsessiveness of the *femmes savantes* cannot be penetrated by verbal subtleties. The bluestockings who advocate dressing up linguistically are, paradoxically, not receptive to verbal persuasion. It takes the artifice of Ariste, in which news is presented factually, without rhetorical adornment, to bring about the marriage.

Le Notaire, Lépine, Julien

The three minor characters are largely dramatic utilities. Nevertheless, their language contributes to the overall comic effect. The Notaire, in the self-satisfied complacency of his belief that he should not change one word of his language echoes the conservatism of Chrysale. But in his preoccupation with the reactions of his peers (his 'compagnons', [1611]), his inability to adjust to the changing situation in front of him, and his solemnly relating to his legal jargon the contrary proposals of Philaminte and Chrysale: 'Deux époux! / C'est trop pour la coutume' (1623-24), he reflects the *femmes savantes.*

The naivety of Lépine's reply to the ingenuously pedantic expressions of Bélise: 'Je m'en suis aperçu, Madame, étant par terre' shows his lack of rhetorical agility. His remark, however, pinpoints the central problem of the play: the gap between (so-called) theory and practice. In his only other speech, his introduction of Vadius, he restricts himself to superficial aspects of character and appearance. He duplicates those whom he serves: his politeness on both occasions belies his feelings.

Julien's appropriation of his master's language (1386-87) is somewhat ambiguous. The effect is laughable whether the speech is interpreted as unconscious imitation or mocking mimicry.

VERSIFICATION

With the exception of Trissotin's two poems, Vadius's letter to Philaminte and Ariste's letters, the play is written in alexandrine verse, in the traditional rhyming couplets with alternating masculine and feminine rhymes. Attention has been drawn to three incomplete lines (760, 771, 1704). Eighteenth-century editors were shocked by what they regarded as negligence on Molière's part and in fact invented speeches to complete the rhyme of 760.[11] The addition was unnecessary and removes the parallelism between the two half lines in this scene, which contributes to its comic structure. The pause allows Trissotin time to make sure that Bélise will not interrupt again and also to recapture the mood of the beginning.

Though the play lacks the imaginative rhyming of *Tartuffe* and *Le Misanthrope,* comic effects are heightened by the verse form.[12] In the final scene, the dignity of Clitandre's language contrasts with the false rhetoric of Trissotin:

> Tout destin avec vous me peut être agréable;
> Tout destin me serait sans vous insupportable.

> (1747-48)

Clitandre's elegant expression (cf. the use of anaphora 'Tout destin' and the antitheses between 'agréable' and 'insupportable' and 'avec vous' and 'sans vous') conveys the depth of his feelings for Henriette, whereas Trissotin's abstractions are an attempt to conceal his self-interest and embarrassment. The repetition of parallel constructions in V, 3 (1625-30) emphasizes the contrast between husband and wife, and Chrysale's abortive attempt to imitate his spouse. Elsewhere,

---

[11] Three variants have been suggested to complete 760: 'PHILAMINTE: Allons, laissons-le lire' (1718); 'ARMANDE: Ecoutons, il va lire' (1733); 'ARMANDE: Ah! laissez-le donc lire' (1730, 34). See *1*, vol. IX, p. 123, n. 4.

[12] For helpful comments on versification see: *46* and C. Bruneau, 'La Langue de Molière' in *Les Femmes savantes,* ed. J. Cordier, Paris, Marcel Didier, 1965, pp. 6-7.

balanced hemistichs convey the discrepancy between Chrysale's illusion of authority and his abject submission to his wife:

PHILAMINTE

Quoi, vous la soutenez?

CHRYSALE

En aucune façon.

MARTINE

Qu'est-ce donc que j'ai fait?

CHRYSALE

Ma foi je ne sais pas.

(433, 445)

Parallelism is sometimes reinforced by the use of stychomythia (one line speech followed by one line speech, two lines by two lines etc.). The slanging match between Trissotin and Vadius is given the momentum of a fencing duel, particularly in view of the quadruple repetition of 'Allez' (1015-18). The verbal combat between Trissotin and Clitandre is an action replay (cf. the use of stychomythia: 1289-92, 1293-1300, 1301-04, 1305-12). The stychomythic duel is reflected in the long and shared fencing metaphor (1314-25) and is worthily crowned by Clitandre's comment on the inequality of the match: 'Autre second, je quitte la partie' (1318).

Comic interruption of a pattern is accentuated by parallelism: see the disproportion between the three synonyms of abuse applied to Clitandre ('Petit sot', 'Le brutal', 'L'impertinent', 1153, 1155, 1157) and their stimuli, Clitandre's reported lack of esteem for Philaminte, his reluctance to praise her, and, most significantly, his failure to appreciate her writing. (The gradation is all the more comic in the context of Clitandre's eavesdropping.)

Comic parallelism is concentrated on the ending of lines: the juxtaposition of 'sciences / expériences' (873-74), 'péripa-

tétisme / platonisme' (877-78), 'physique / politique' (893-94)
enhances our view of the automatic use of pedantic terminology. The combination of dissonant words can undermine
argument: 'esclave asservi / philosophie' (43-44), 'animale /
ravale' (47-48), 'femmes sensibles / pauvretés horribles'
(51-52), or make the attack more barbed: 'étoffe / philosophe'
(55-56), 'élévations / spéculations' (57-58). The association of
'Trissotin' and 'latin' (four times) and 'larcins' and 'Latins'
establishes a comic link between the poet and Latin and lack
of originality, i.e. plagiarism (see *46*, p. 154, n. 17).

The proximity of related words with antithetical meanings translates in epigrammatic form the pedant's folly. Such
lines as:

> Raisonner est l'emploi de toute ma maison
> Et le raisonnement en bannit la raison [...]
>
> Et j'ai des serviteurs, et ne suis point servi [...]
>
> Qu'un sot savant est sot plus qu'un sot ignorant.
>
> (597-98, 602, 1296)

have proved as memorable as any in Molière's plays. Comic
effect is also achieved by the incongruity between verse form
and content: e.g. between the servant's popular speech and
the formality of the alexandrine (1641-44, see *46*, p. 149) or
the quintuple dislocation of 776, which conveys a breathless,
uncultured response to a stanza of Trissotin's sonnet.

NAMES

Molière's choice of names emphasizes the fantasy element. Several are drawn from the literary tradition. Chrysale
and Philaminte and Ariste are derived from a tradition which
goes back to the Italian Renaissance and even to classical
sources. To the same category belong Dorante, Damis,
Cléonte and Lysidas whom Bélise designates as her lovers,

Argante and Damon, the two bankers mentioned by Ariste, and Iris, Philis and Amarante at whom Henriette pokes fun (see *37,* p. 266).

The names of characters anticipate their roles. Semantically, Ariste signifies 'very good'; Chrysale means 'gold', and is glossed almost tautologically by the description 'bon bourgeois', one who is very well-off – hence the connection with Henriette as a trophy for Trissotin and the preparation of the denouement which works by apparent cancellation of the gold. The ironic associations of Trissotin's name (thrice 'sot') are evoked by Clitandre in 1337-38. The nickname Lépine suggests the tall, lean, but ungainly servant of farce. The etymology of Philaminte is less obvious: 'Phil' signifies love of; 'aminte' may have been taken from *Aminta,* Tasso's hedonistic pastoral drama (1573): this would suggest both her inordinate attachment to literature and poets, and the unreal world she mentally inhabits. Phonetically, Argante, the banker, calls to mind 'argent' and the root of Clitandre is probably 'tendre', which is appropriate for the true lover of the play. Bélise's manner of speaking may be indicated by her name: the word *bêler* ('bleat') in its figurative sense signifies to speak in a silly, plaintive, bleating voice. The popularity or rarity of the characters' names suggests comic contrasts. Armande was considered elegant at the time (Molière parodies the pseudo-refinement of the role) while Henriette had become popular since the time of Henriette de France and Henriette d'Angleterre, having been a noble name in the Middle Ages (see *37,* p. 266). Martine was thought of as plebeian, while Julien was more distinguished. The latinized endings of Vadius and of the *savants* Rasius and Baldus give an aura of pedantry to the roles. Ironically, the Greek specialists have Latin names while the names of three of the bourgeois (Chrysale, Ariste and Philaminte) are derived from the Greek.

4

Ideas

INTELLECTUAL problems have caused more ink to flow
than any other aspect of the play. Critical focus has shown,
paradoxically, a lack of perspective which would no doubt
have amused the great comic dramatist, who was not averse
to putting his critics on stage and to extracting from their
misapprehensions material for comedy! Criticism has been
dogged by attempts to find Molière's attitude to one of the
major themes, the education of women. Many have followed
the line of the nineteenth-century critic Faguet who identified Molière with Chrysale as an advocate of the Paris
bourgeoisie. It seems absurd to equate Molière with a character who is hen-pecked and an ignoramus, and who would
confine women (and their conversation) to household matters. If the ideas of Chrysale were put into practice in the
seventeenth century we would not now be reading the work
of Mme de Sévigné, Mme de Lafayette, Mme de Maintenon
or Mlle de Scudéry.

Others have opted for Clitandre and Henriette as the
dramatist's *porte-parole*. Though the lovers represent the
norm of the play, it is a comic and dramatic norm, and not
one on which Molière invites us to meditate. Besides, Clitandre's moderate and unpedantic ideal was by no means original and has been traced to Mlle de Scudéry and La Mothe Le
Vayer (see *27*, p. 200). Recent studies have viewed the play as
a feminist tract and have shown great sympathy for Molière's
comic heroines and hostility towards the representatives of
the bourgeois mentality which 'imprisoned women in the
home'. The sexist interpretation is, however, anachronistic.
The context of the play is social and not professional – the
femmes savantes are not going out to look for a job! No

protest was made in the seventeenth century about the treatment of women in the play. It was over fifty years after the first performance that the first accusation of anti-feminism was levelled (see *52*, p. 25). Furthermore, the ideas voiced in the play are found in other comedies of the time, notably Samuel Chappuzeau's *Le Cercle des femmes* (1656) and *L'Académie des femmes* (1661). Judged by the criterion of a social and moral thesis, the play would be banal.

One of the most common mistakes is to confuse Molière's heroines with real seventeenth-century *savantes*. Molière's disclaimer regarding the distinction between the true and the false in the preface to *Les Précieuses ridicules* and the *Premier placet* of *Tartuffe* could well have been applied to *Les Femmes savantes*:

> [...] les plus excellentes choses sont sujettes à être copiées par de mauvais singes qui méritent d'être bernés [...]

> Je n'ai point laissé d'équivoque, j'ai ôté ce qui pouvait confondre le bien avec le mal, et ne me suis servi dans cette peinture que des couleurs expresses et des traits essentiels qui font connaître d'abord un véritable et franc hypocrite.

To say that Molière is attacking women's aspirations to learning is to fall into the error of the *femmes savantes* who mistake appearances for reality and accept at face value Trissotin's and Vadius's semblance of erudition.

The audience of Molière's day had many examples of genuine scholarship amongst women. Queen Christina of Sweden was able to speak four or five languages and was visited by numerous scholars. Anne-Marie de Schurmann had mastered most known modern languages in addition to Hebrew, Greek, Arabic and Latin, and was an able mathematician and theologian, as well as an artist and sculptor. Women were receiving instruction on diverse academic subjects – albeit, in a popularized and edulcorated form: Louis de Lesclache held classes in philosophy three times a week for society ladies and courtiers; women attended the lectures on philosophy and science given by Rohault, Régis, Sauveur and

Duverny; Malebranche directed a learned gathering on Cartesian ethics and metaphysics which included Mme de Grignan, Mme de Bonnevaut, Mlle de La Vigne, Mlle Descartes (niece of the philosopher), and Mlle de Wailly; Mme de La Sablière's house was frequented by the physicist Roberval, the mathematician Sauveur, the orientalist Herbelot, the traveller and amateur philosopher Bernier; Mme de Sévigné and Mme de Lafayette were taught by Ménage; in the Académie of the abbé d'Aubignac were seen 'plusieurs personnes de qualité de l'un et de l'autre sexe'. These truly educated women would have given the audience a historical perspective against which to view the behaviour and pronouncements of all the characters. Molière's audience perceived the distinction between the reality of the play and actuality. Truly educated women did not feel victimized: they would not have considered themselves *érudites* or *savantes*. Mme de Sévigné went so far as to commend the author for a 'fort plaisante pièce'.

I do not propose to deal further with the social, intellectual and literary movements of the latter part of the seventeenth century. This ground has already been very adequately covered (see *6, 27, 29, 32* and *52*). My aim in this chapter is to examine the comic and dramatic use of intellectual aspects of the problems raised in the play: erudition versus ignorance, marriage and the family, and social climbing.

ERUDITION VERSUS IGNORANCE

Vanity and egoism motivate both the pursuit of knowledge and the preservation of ignorance. Philaminte will not stop at equality with men but dreams of superiority in the battle of the sexes. Learning – like her proposed reforms of language – is a means to that end. Anyone who does not flatter her work is censured (e.g. 1137-38). Armande cultivates intellectual activities to assert authority over her sister. Bélise appropriates to herself everything she reads, sees or hears, and convinces herself she is worthy of being idolized by all men. Trissotin and Vadius are introduced to give celebrity to the ladies, while they themselves turn their knowledge to selfish ends – to literary conceit and in Trissotin's case to the pursuit of a dowry.

Chrysale's condemnation of the acquisition of knowledge is, however, also based on self-interest: 'On ne sait comme va mon pot dont j'ai besoin [...] L'un me brûle mon rot en lisant quelque histoire, / L'autre rêve à des vers quand je demande à boire' (594, 599-600). Both pedants and conservatives take their views to extremes. The ladies' quest for knowledge is not ridiculous in itself. Comedy arises from their desire to know everything about everything and to think this possible – about physics, astronomy, ancient languages as well as 'le bon usage', in fact, to surpass the encyclopaedic knowledge of the most learned blue-stocking. Ironically, such pedantry was condemned by one of the leading female writers of the time, whose *précieux* language the *femmes savantes* try to imitate:

> Encore que je voulusse que les femmes sussent plus de choses qu'elles n'en savent pour l'ordinaire, je ne veux pourtant jamais qu'elles agissent ni qu'elles parlent en savantes. Je veux donc bien qu'on puisse dire d'une personne de mon sexe qu'elle sait cent choses dont elle ne se vante pas, qu'elle a l'esprit fort éclairé, qu'elle connaît finement les beaux ouvrages, qu'elle parle bien, qu'elle écrit juste et qu'elle sait le monde, mais je ne veux pas qu'on puisse dire d'elle: C'est une femme savante [...] Ce n'est pas que celle qu'on n'appellera point savante ne puisse savoir autant et plus de choses que celle à qui on donnera ce terrible nom, mais c'est qu'elle se sait mieux servir de son esprit, et qu'elle sait cacher adroitement ce que l'autre montre mal à propos. (Cited in *1*, IX, pp. 72-73, n. 3)

Chrysale's philistinism is as ludicrous as his wife's pedantry. He dismisses all that is above his head, and would have all books burned except a large Plutarch (which was useful for pressing his 'rabats'). Martine's remarks on the evil of books and advocacy of illiteracy (1666) is similarly absurd.

The unsystematized knowledge of the *femmes savantes* comically reveals their ignorance. In III, 2, their discussion moves without transition from one subject to another, culminating in Armande's *omnium gatherum:* 'physique, / Grammaire, histoire, vers, morale et politique' (why stop there?). Trissotin's professed love of 'péripatétisme' (Aristotelian logic) is vitiated by his failure to pursue an argument with any rigour. Philaminte's appropriation of the fifth book of Plato's *Republic* (848) is ironic, in that her source describes an imaginary city 'with equal rights (and especially duties) for men and women' (6, p. 194). Philaminte will admit only women and poets (the latter were banned from Plato's utopia!). Interest in Cartesian cosmology: 'matière subtile', 'l'aimant', 'tourbillons', 'mondes tombants' is caricatured by the claim to have observed men and steeples on the moon (889-92). Curiosity about the nature of the moon's surface is not comic in itself – the recent discovery of the telescope (the bluestockings have installed one!, [565-66]) had brought a new awareness in astronomy. But the dogmatism ('clairement', 'tout comme je vous vois') and the descent from the technical to plain narrative make the claims ridiculous.

The *femmes savantes*' vague eclecticism verges on the nonsensical. Epicurus's dogmatism (popularized by Gassendi in the seventeenth century) is combined with Descartes's 'vortices' and unspecified branches of philosophy (44-45, 1146-47). Bélise synthesizes Epicurus's materialistic atomism with the idealistic 'matière subtile' of Descartes. Her preference for the latter is due to an imaginary fear of the concept of the vacuum in nature, a concept which she has failed to comprehend. Similarly, in her theory of gravity, she applies to movement what is true only of something static (742). Her love of science matches her romantic delusions. The comic effect depends not only on the garbled account but also, as Hall has suggested, on sexual innuendoes of words like 'petits corps', 'vide', and 'matière subtile' (20, p. 95). Philaminte oscillates between Plato's metaphysics, Cartesian physics, and Stoic ethics.

Chrysale's and Martine's ideology is more systematized but is reasoned in a very illogical manner. Chrysale's long tirade in II, 7 is full of non-sequiturs as he commends the *modus vivendi* of his forebears. His equation of enjoyment of

life and the absence of reading material matches the simplis-
tic and half-baked notions of philosophy of the ladies, all the
more so, as it is reformulated in a lower register by Martine
in Act V. The gap between theory and practice enhances the
comedy. Chrysale's abortive attempts to implement the credo
of his ancestors parallel the coterie's inability to live out the
Stoic ideal. Armande's and Trissotin's self-contradictions
have been dealt with elsewhere. Philaminte's irascibility,
minatory tone, and spiteful attitude to Clitandre and Vadius
are far removed from the serenity ('ataraxia') advocated by
her exemplar, the sage Zeno. Philaminte's stoicism is however portrayed ambivalently at the end (one sees once again
her superiority over Armande and Bélise). Molière's comic
protagonists are not usually pasteboard types, ridiculous in
every respect. His defence of the 'contradictory' portrayal of
Arnolphe (*La Critique de L'Ecole des femmes,* sc. 6) could
well be applied to Philaminte (almost without modification!):
'il n'est pas incompatible qu'une personne soit ridicule en de
certaines choses et honnête homme en d'autres'.

The mental blindness of the coterie conflicts with their
pretentions to knowledge. All their intensive cultivation of
mind over body does not allow them to see through Trissotin's duplicity. True learning would have given insight into
the sonnet's true worth, and also into Trissotin's plagiarism
(the ladies have to be apprised of it by Vadius and even then
they cannot accept his warning). They welcome Trissotin
merely because he is a 'bel esprit', and receive Vadius on
Trissotin's recommendation. Trissotin for his part is unable
to see through Ariste's ruse in V, 4. The coterie is as
unenlightened as Chrysale, who is even uncurious about
Clitandre's presence in the house and who dismisses Trissotin
as merely a fool, failing to perceive the more duplicitous
dowry-hunter he turns out to be. The median path between
mock-erudition and ignorance, represented by Clitandre and
Henriette, is part of the comic framework. Henriette's anti-
intellectualism is calculated to taunt Armande and to avoid
the attentions of Trissotin. Ironically, she has a better grasp of
ideas than the *femmes savantes* (cf. her awareness of precious
literature in V, 1) and conforms to the image of Clitandre's

ideal woman, who is counselled to pretend to be ignorant of matters with which she is familiar:

> Et j'aime que souvent aux questions qu'on fait,
> Elle sache ignorer les choses qu'elle sait.

(221-22)

Clitandre's attitude to learning and to the education of women has been misinterpreted by modern feminists, who have not taken into account the dramatic context or the historical perspective. Clitandre is reacting against ostentation and pedantry, against failure to relate learning to life. He himself is not unfamiliar with ancient philosophical ideals, witness his evaluation of the Platonic distinction between body and soul in IV, 3. He does not advocate, like Chrysale, that women devote themselves exclusively to domestic issues, and does not put his knowledge to selfish ends. While derivative, his liberalism ('Je consens qu'une femme ait des clartés de tout') is in advance of some of the more repressive theories of the time. Less than three years after *Les Femmes savantes,* Poulain de la Barre, in his *De l'excellence des hommes contre l'égalité des sexes,* published a justification of male superiority (see *6,* p. 22), and Fénelon's treatise on the intellectual training of women (*L'Education des filles,* 1687) hardly goes beyond Clitandre's declarations. However, Clitandre's views are pragmatic rather than propositional, and are related to the dramatic situation. Moreover, the paradoxical attitude of learned ignorance was part of a long-standing comic tradition, explored notably in the sixteenth century by François Rabelais.

MARRIAGE AND THE FAMILY

The norm is again set by the lovers, who adopt a natural attitude to sex and marriage. Conventional duties and responsibilities are upheld (15-16), but their reciprocal trust, generosity and self-denial produces what has been described as the most explicitly romantic vision of marriage in all of Molière (see *25*, p. 93). The bluestockings' usurpation of authority in the household is portrayed ironically. In her reaction against the traditional views of marriage and the family and in her nomination of Trissotin, Philaminte assumes the role of the heavy father – who, ironically, is the main butt of her criticism. Her philosophy of liberation and her campaign for women's rights lead to a reign of terror, in which, paradoxically, she sacrifices two of her own sex, Martine and Henriette. Molière's audience would not have taken seriously Philaminte's inversion of the social norm, particularly as the part was played by the male actor Hubert. Although travesty in the seventeenth-century theatre did not provoke the same hilarity as nowadays, yet the fact that the part of a woman who had usurped the role of a man was played by a man gives further comic emphasis to the unnaturalness of Philaminte's pretensions.

Armande's anti-matrimonial attitude, if followed rigorously, would lead to depopulation, as Henriette deduces (77-78). Furthermore, Armande's choice of celibacy is revoked in IV, 2. Her subsequent resumption of the Platonic disguise is merely a device to save face after Clitandre's rejection. Armande's views on marriage are drawn from *précieux* novels (see her terminology in the first two scenes). Comedy is provoked by her refusal to distinguish between literature and life (until it is too late), and by her failure to comprehend (as in matters of science and philosophy) the fundamentals of the *précieux* movement: her attempt to prolong courtship indefinitely – which is the reason Clitandre switches his attention to Henriette – goes against the code by which courtship would eventually lead to marriage; out of jealousy, Armande betrays the idealism of the *précieuses* in upholding a tradition which the heroines of Mlle de Scudéry were united in combatting – marriages without love and the tyranny of parental choice:

> Sachez que le devoir vous soumet à leurs lois,
> Qu'il ne vous est permis d'aimer que par leur choix,
> Qu'ils ont sur votre cœur l'autorité suprême,
> Et qu'il est criminel d'en disposer vous-même...

Nous devons obéir, ma sœur, à nos parents;
Une mère[13] a sur nous une entière puissance,
Et vous croyez en vain par votre résistance....

(165-68, 1096-98)

Bélise's 'Platonic promiscuity', derived from her misreading of gallant literature, is a grotesque self-delusion. It is significant that the two who pronounce most on love and marriage are in no position to claim objectivity. The ironic presentation of the 'emancipated' view of marriage is completed by Trissotin's mercenary attitude and bland acceptance of potential cuckoldry. Chrysale's abdication of his status of paterfamilias and his cowering behind the servant would have been equally ridiculous to the seventeenth-century audience. Chrysale's vision of a 'totally domesticated' wife is a *reductio ad absurdum* of the traditional attitude. He chooses to live in an imaginary world of the past, in which his authority would never be questioned. As for the problem of enforced marriages in the play, Molière has frequently been considered as a campaigner against excessive restraint and lack of choice. Though rooted in social reality, the enforced marriage in the play is a topos of comic plot construction which features in many of his plays[14] and which goes back to Plautus and Terence.

SOCIAL CLIMBING

The bluestockings' aspirations to social elevation correspond to their desire for intellectual ascendancy. They dissociate themselves from anything they regard as bourgeois. Armande declares that marriage is only for those of 'low breeding' and of 'vulgar taste', while Bélise wonders if she is of the same middle-class stock as her brother Chrysale

[13] In the social reality, it was of course *un père*! (cf. l. 1105.)
[14] Cf. *Le Médecin volant, Les Précieuses ridicules, Sganarelle ou le Cocu imaginaire, L'Ecole des femmes, Tartuffe, L'Avare, Le Bourgeois gentilhomme, Le Malade imaginaire.*

(616-19) – the audience is in no doubt! The ladies' enthusiasm for Trissotin's sonnet is inspired, in part, by their being told that it had been praised by a 'princesse' and a 'duchesse'. Moreover, Philaminte tries to turn her bourgeois home into an aristocratic salon. Although bourgeois salons had increased in number after the wars of the Fronde (1648-1653), the type of salon which the bluestockings are trying to imitate is nearer to the upper-class model of the *chambre bleue* of the Marquise de Rambouillet which functioned from 1620 until the Marquise's death in 1665, but which was particularly renowned from 1625 to 1648 for its genuine and not unsuccessful attempts to rise above the crudeness of contemporary society in the matter of language and manners. Philaminte's imitation of such salons, together with her idolatry of Vaugelas, ironically aligns her with the husband she so despises: both attempt to re-create an age which is past and for which they are ill-equipped.

The *femmes savantes*' ludicrous imitation of nobility also echoes Monsieur Jourdain's futile efforts to ape 'les gens de qualité'. The ladies' pedantry would have been ill-received in high society and would have exposed them for what they are: bourgeoises – witness Mlle de Scudéry's condemnation of the *femme savante,* the horror of pedantry on the part of one of the characters in *La Prétieuse* by the abbé de Pure, and the *précieuse* in Boileau's *10e Satire* who scorns the frivolous lovers of Greek and Latin (see *6* and *8,* but beware of the latter's identification of Clitandre with Molière). The bluestockings are oblivious to the distinction between aristocratic *préciosité* and pedantry.

Paradoxically, the true social elevation sought by the *femmes savantes* is attainable through the marriage of Henriette to Clitandre, the gentleman who moves in Court circles. Armande fails to take her chance of a change in social status. And Philaminte's support of Trissotin makes her inimical to the Court, the highest seat of nobility. The female pedants' failure to recognize in Clitandre the true *honnête homme* (the man of good taste and breeding) further reveals their blindness, and recalls the unwillingness of Cathos and Magdelon in *Les Précieuses ridicules* to recognize that the sophisticated lovers they had been seeking were the very ones they had rejected, La Grange and Du Croisy. The comic incongruity of the *femmes savantes'* social climbing is enriched by Chrysale's and Martine's complacency and lack of ambition to rise above their actual mediocrity. As in the matter of the education of women and the question of marriage, it seems fruitless to speculate on the particular sympathies of Molière with regard to the class structure. The theme of 'social climbing' offers a source of some of the conflicts, and a backcloth with which the audience of the time, drawn primarily from the *honnêtes gens,* was most familiar.

5

Satire

W H I L E there is insufficient evidence to postulate particular models for the *femmes savantes,* Molière's public and most editors have identified, as sources for Trissotin and Vadius, two writers, the abbé Cotin (1604-82) and Ménage (1613-92). The former was a preacher at Court and a member of the Académie Française who knew Latin, Greek, Hebrew and Syriac. The latter taught Spanish, Italian and Latin to Mme de Sévigné and Mme de Lafayette, and under the latinized name of Aegidius Menagius published a vast collection of poems called *Poemata.*

The allusions to Corin are more obvious than the references to Ménage. Trissotin's sonnet and epigram are taken verbatim – apart from a few minor changes and two errors of transcription [15] – from Cotin's work. In addition, if one can trust the *Ménagiana,* La Thorillière, the actor playing Trissotin, wore the old *soutane* of the abbé Cotin, which Molière would have perhaps procured from a second-hand clothes dealer. According to contemporary evidence the play was originally entitled *Tricotin* (see *2,* II, p. 1464, n. 7).

The association of Vadius with Ménage is deduced mainly from Clitandre's attack on the distribution of court 'pensions' (IV, 3) and the quarrel between Vadius and Trissotin (III, 3). Ménage and Cotin received annual 'pensions' of 2000 *livres*

---

[15] Cotin's *Sonnet à Mlle de Longueville, à présent duchesse de Nemours sur sa fièvre quarte* becomes *Sonnet à la Princesse Uranie sur sa fièvre* (the name *Princesse Uranie* is, however, found at the head of Cotin's other poems); *Sur un Carrosse de couleur amarante acheté pour une Dame* is rendered *Sur un Carrosse de couleur amarante, donné à une dame de ses amies; Et jour et nuit* is transcribed *Et nuit et jour,* and *Qu'il me coûte* is transcribed *Qu'il m'en coûte.*

and 1200 *livres* respectively from 1663 until 1667, when they were suddenly struck off the list. The quarrel in III, 3 is said to have been based on a real dispute between Ménage and Cotin which had arisen some eight years before the première of *Les Femmes savantes* from an alleged slight given to Mlle de Scudéry by Cotin, when the latter read his sonnet *Sur sa fièvre quarte* to the Duchesse de Nemours. The offence was avenged by Ménage in an insulting epigram, to which Cotin and his friends replied in a collection of defamatory verse published under the title of *La Ménagerie* and dedicated to Mlle de Scudéry. The venue of the quarrel seems to be in doubt, with the salon of Mme de Montpensier and the home of Gilles Boileau being advanced by different sources.

Molière may have been inspired by the historical event. But, as editors have pointed out, he had to hand a theatrical source in Saint-Evremond's *Comédie des Académistes,* in which two academicians, Godeau and Colletet, first congratulate each other and then quarrel vehemently. He may also have drawn on his own play, *La Critique de L'Ecole des femmes,* in which an author's obsession with the public reading of his work is central to the plot. Dorante anticipates the quarrel between Vadius and Trissotin:

> Ce serait une chose plaisante à mettre sur le théâtre que [les] grimaces savantes [des auteurs] et leurs raffinements ridicules, leur vicieuse coutume d'assassiner les gens dans leurs ouvrages, leur friandise de louange, leurs lignes offensives et défensives, aussi bien que leurs guerres d'esprit et leurs combats de prose et de vers.   (sc. 6)

Other possible sources include *Le Bourgeois gentilhomme,* II, 3 (see *42,* p. 357), or the quarrel between Alceste and Oronte in *Le Misanthrope,* I, 2.

The personal circumstances which are thought to have led up to Molière's attack on the abbé Cotin are well-documented. In his *Satire des Satires* (published anonymously in 1666) Cotin uses Boileau's admiration for Molière as an example of poor taste and also criticizes the dramatist's work directly:

> J'ai vu de mauvais vers sans blâmer le poète.
> J'ai lu ceux de Molière, et ne l'ai point sifflé.

Cotin took sides against Molière in the quarrel surrounding one of the dramatist's early successes, *L'Ecole des femmes* (1662), and seems to have preached against his *Tartuffe* (eventually published in 1669). Cotin's verbal campaign against Molière and Boileau continued in 1667 in another work which he published anonymously under the title *La Critique désintéressée sur les satires du temps* in which he inveighs against le Sieur des Vipéreaux (Boileau) and accuses comic dramatists of atheism. Boileau avenged himself for the attack in his *9e Satire,* and, it is thought, may have prevailed upon his close friend to get embroiled in the dispute through *Les Femmes savantes.*

According to Donneau de Visé, the play's first reviewer, Molière had disclaimed all personal allusions two days before the first performance and had warned us of the danger of looking for real persons in his comedy. Molière's advice was no doubt prudential, intended not least to placate Mlle de Scudéry. Cotin found the cap fitted too well and was greatly offended. Ménage was astute enough not to recognize his portrait in Vadius and compiled a laudatory epitaph on the occasion of Molière's death. His pupil, Mme de Sévigné, we have seen, spoke well of the play.

Molière has been pilloried for his attacks on Cotin – mainly by critics like Voltaire who, somewhat ironically, was not renowned for his generosity towards adversaries. At a biographical level, the picture of a cruel and vindictive Molière which has been drawn from his supposed portrayal of Cotin does not accord with the overall view presented by those who knew him best. Only three of his troupe are known to have left him: René Berthelot's temporary defection was caused by Jodelet's joining the troupe in 1659, Brécourt's move to the Hôtel de Bourgogne was probably due to personal ambition, and Mlle du Parc's departure was brought about more by the attentions of the rival dramatist Racine than by disaffection with Molière. And Molière's willingness to put

his life second to the needs of the staff of his theatre is
captured in remarks he is reported to have made just before
his death: 'Il y a cinquante pauvres ouvriers qui n'ont que
leur journée pour vivre: que feront-ils si l'on ne joue pas?'[16]

It is easy to become lost in the historical and biographical
detail and miss the imaginative element in the roles of both
Trissotin and Vadius. Molière makes Trissotin a pedant as
well as a 'bel esprit' (Cotin was not a pedant); a dowry-
hunter, an essential ingredient of the plot (Cotin, as a priest,
could not have had such interests); a relatively young man,
perhaps in his thirties (Cotin in 1672 was 68); an impostor
and a parasite. The poetry which Molière lifts from Cotin's is
among his worst. Molière could have borrowed it for aesthetic reasons. In the dramatic context in which he places
Cotin's poems, Molière extracts sexual innuendo which the
author would almost certainly not have intended. Viewed in
the totality of the scene and of the play, Cotin's second-rate
literature is transformed – paradoxically – into a work of art.

Plagiarism of Cotin's work is also related to the theme of
disguise and pretence. The audience's awareness of the bor-
rowing gives further irony to Trissotin's claims to originality.
Literary imposture takes the ladies' intellectual pretensions
one stage further. The *femmes savantes'* imitation is inade-
quate, while Trissotin's is servile. Molière mocks the ladies'
gullibility in failing to recognize Trissotin's literary charlatanism (the truly educated man, Clitandre, is all too aware of
regurgitation – not merely in the poem!). The ladies' mechanical responses are even more ironic given the banal and
derivative nature of Trissotin's poetry.

The ironic perspective is enhanced by Molière's blend of
theatrical illusion and reality. Vadius's 'Peut-on rien voir
d'égal aux sonnets que vous faites?' (978) and Philaminte's
claim that criticism is legitimate 'Pourvu qu'à la personne on
ne s'attaque pas' (1320) give irony to Molière's disclaimer
two days before the production. There is comic deception of
expectations when Trissotin and Vadius send each other not

to the devil, but to the 'devil's surrogate, Boileau' (1026-27). It is also ironic that Molière transfers to Vadius's prose letter read out by Philaminte Cotin's accusations of plagiarism against Ménage in the *Œuvres galantes* and the *Ménagerie* (see 6, p. 201, note to 1394).

The choice of *Tricotin* (later *Trissotin*) as a title for the play can be explained in terms of the dramatic function of the role. Like Tartuffe, who comes on at the same juncture in Act III, he poses the main obstacle to the hopes of the lovers. And it is his come-uppance that the audience anticipates in the denouement.

Vadius's role too transcends the circumstantial, and can also be justified in terms of the overall structure of the play. Molière's introduction of a second pedant probably goes back to *Les Précieuses ridicules,* in which Jodelet is brought on to complete the caricature of the *précieuses.* Vadius's role also adds to the symmetry of the play (see chapter 7). Whatever its inspiration, the quarrel amplifies the comic deflation of pretentiousness.

Molière's satire in this play is somewhat double-edged. There may be a personal element in it: in the present state of knowledge, without correspondence from the author to guide us, we cannot be sure of Molière's real intentions. The comedy, however, remains. What is of particular interest from a dramatic point of view is the way Molière subordinates allusions made to real people to the plays into which he has incorporated them. The real is transformed by his artistic imagination into a further illusion. To the modern audience, what Cotin and Ménage represent is more important than what they were actually like as people. Cotin, nowadays, is largely forgotten. But Trissotin lives on!

6

Source and Genre

T H E theatrical sources upon which Molière drew have
been well established: Calderon, Desmarets de Saint-Sorlin,
Saint-Evremond and Chappuzeau. However, as in other
comedies of the later period (notably *George Dandin* [1668],
which is a reworking of one of his early *canevas, La Jalousie
du Barbouillé*), Molière's primary source is his own corpus.
Les Femmes savantes is to some extent a reworking of
aspects of Molière's first success in Paris, *Les Précieuses
ridicules,* within the framework of one of his most controver-
sial plays, *Tartuffe.* Some of the roles from *Les Précieuses* are
developed in our play: Armande is an amalgam of Cathos
and Magdelon, the two 'pecques provinciales' who try to
imitate Parisian *préciosité*; Chrysale has traces of the earthy
Gorgibus (whose name is aptly almost an anagram of bourgeois); Martine recalls the maid Marotte, who also protests
against the jargon of her mistresses; Clitandre develops the
honnête lovers, La Grange and Du Croisy whose qualities are
not appreciated by the girls; the sonneteer Trissotin has traits
of the clever valet Mascarille, who impersonates a marquis to
impress his all too easily deceived female audience; Vadius,
we have seen, corresponds to Jodelet. Roles added to *Les
Femmes savantes* are the mother, Philaminte, the aunt and
uncle, Bélise and Ariste, and the lover, Henriette. The main
theme, too, has undergone a change – from false *préciosité* to
pedantry.

The plot of *Les Précieuses* was too insubstantial for a
five-act comedy. Molière has incorporated material from
Tartuffe, the play he was working on at the time *Les Femmes
savantes* is thought to have been conceived. Orgon (the male
version of Philaminte) plans to marry his daughter Mariane

(Henriette in embryo), against her inclinations, to Tartuffe (a religious Trissotin) as a kind of insurance against eternal perdition. A kindly uncle, Cléante, intervenes on behalf of the lovers, Mariane and Valère, but unlike his future counterpart Ariste, has no success. The happy ending of *Tartuffe* is secured by the arrival of the king's messenger, a character who does not appear till the final act.

Only the role of Bélise is missing. Her dramatic antecedents are Hespérie of Desmarets, the eccentric aunt of Thomas Corneille's *Le Baron d'Albikrak* (6, p. 48), Molière's doctor figures, and Mme Pernelle.

GENRE

Until recently, *Les Femmes savantes* had not suffered the fate of many of Molière's comedies which have been regarded as tragic. Even the Romantics in their sombre re-evaluation of Molière's work, failed to discern any tragic quality.[17] In the last forty years, however, the play has increasingly been viewed as a 'drame bourgeois'. I have tried to show that this interpretation is misguided in view of the comic language and rhythm of the play (see chapters 2 and 3). The piece has also been considered to be one of Molière's most literary comedies. The romanesque complexity, seen in the double triangle referred to in chapter 1, gives a degree of sophistication absent in some of Molière's later works. The creation of two sisters takes us back to one of his earliest plays, *Le Dépit amoureux,* which was constructed after the literary tradition. The idea of rivalry between sisters in *Les Femmes savantes* is however an innovation in Molière's plays, though it is common in the erudite tradition of the Italian Renaissance. The large discursive element and the fact that *Les Femmes savantes* was written in five acts and in verse shows a

---

[17] Except for one critic, Jules Janin. For an account of the play's reception over the last three hundred years see: J. K. Robinson, 'French Critical Opinion of Molière's *Les Femmes savantes* (1672-1968)', Columbia University, 1970, DAI 1970/71, 2963 A.

departure from the pattern followed by Molière after *Le Misanthrope* in 1666 (with the exception of *Tartuffe,* which was originally conceived in 1664) and emphasizes its literary form.

An attempt has been made to identify the play with *comédie-ballet,* a genre to which Molière had devoted his attention almost exclusively at the time of composing *Les Femmes savantes* (see *17*). However interesting this thesis may be, the difficulty lies in the fact that some of the techniques enumerated, such as repetition and symmetry, are common to other genres. There has been a general reluctance to admit to elements of farce in the play. Farce has often been regarded as beneath the attention of the critic, though there is no reason why this should be so. It is true that *Les Femmes savantes* is far removed from the seemingly plotless *canevas* which Molière had created at the beginning of his career as a dramatist. It is also true that the slapstick element is more limited than in other plays: Lépine's fall, the greeting of Vadius 'pour l'amour du grec', and the arrival of Julien, weighed down by a pile of books. But the subject matter and some of the traits of character derive from the far-fetched, topsy-turvy world of farce.

The subject matter had been touched on in two medieval farces: *Les Femmes qui se font passer maîtresses,* and *Les Femmes qui apprenent à parler latin* (in which three Parisian ladies each learn to speak Latin, one after the other). [18] Chrysale's situation vis-à-vis his wife reminds us of the conjugal power struggles in Old French farce between the weak and peace-loving *mal-marié* and his assertive, querulous wife. In medieval farce, the conflict centres on the struggle to determine who will be master in the house. The wife is usually of higher class than the husband. In *Les Femmes savantes,* the social inequality is imaginary (Philaminte and Bélise think they belong to a superior rank). Martine alerts the audience to the parallel between Chrysale and the *mal-marié* by her reference to 'le jocrisse' (1649), the

---

[18] See Barbara C. Bowen, 'Some Elements of French Farce in Molière', *Esprit Créateur,* VI (Fall, 1966), p. 169.

hen-pecked husband of the Farce. The parody of the authority of the head of the house is reinforced by the travesty. Philaminte's opening scene can be compared to the farcical expository scene in *Tartuffe,* in which Mme Pernelle, also played by Hubert in drag, rebukes everyone in sight for trivial offences.

The farcical theme of cuckoldry does not in itself feature in the play, if one interprets 'cuckoldry' merely in the literal sense. (The sexual problem is not raised directly: one feels that that side of things is long over between Chrysale and Philaminte.) But Chrysale's long speech (558 ff.) is exactly like a lover's lament over the unfaithfulness of his mistress, sexual favours being metaphorically replaced by domestic duties. Chrysale feels that in abandoning these for the pursuit of 'learning', Philaminte has deserted him and, in that sense, played him false. Metaphorical cuckoldry is also implied in the sensual reception of Trissotin's poems (in which Trissotin and Philaminte are regarded as 'père' and 'mère'). Molière transposes the cuckoldry theme (cf. *George Dandin*) from the sexual to the domestic sphere. The basis of this aspect is rooted in farce. The role of Chrysale shows traits of the Capitan, the coward of the Italian farce tradition, the *commedia dell'arte,* who is always boasting of what he imagines he has done, or will do. Chrysale does not share the Capitan's claim to military valour (the *miles gloriosus* tradition). But the braggart's boast of illegitimate children is captured in Chrysale's 'fredaines'.

The doctor figures of Molière's farces, derived in turn from the *dottore* of the *commedia dell'arte,* have provided aspects of both male and female pedants in *Les Femmes savantes.* Vadius's costume ('vêtu de noir'), which evokes the doctor's gown, gives a comic anticipation of the pedant role, which Vadius's unwarranted use of Greek and display of learning fulfills. His denunciation of the verbiage of his fellow pedants resembles the doctor's wordy praise of brevity in *La Jalousie du Barbouillé,* sc. 6. Trissotin combines traits of the pedant with those of the scheming valet and those of the villain of farce.

The *femmes savantes* are female doctors who discourse glibly on such diverse matters as philosophy, astronomy, literature and grammar. The only subject from the *dottore*'s repertoire not included is medicine. The bluestockings' obsessive preoccupation with the form of their interlocutors' remarks, their repeated claims to distinction and desire for admiration, and the comic irrelevancy of Bélise's verbiage, are further characteristics of Molière's doctors.

The play contains no *coups de bâton,* the stock business of farce. However, Martine sanctions wife-beating, and the quarrel between the pedants in III, 3 amounts to verbal fisticuffs. Witticisms, which are less common in literary comedy than in farce, are exploited in the equivocal use of language in the sonnet scene, and in Martine's puns (492, 495-96) which can be compared with wordplay in *La Jalousie du Barbouillé,* sc. 2.[19] Such linguistic jokes tend to be rather gratuitous in farce, but in *Les Femmes savantes,* they illustrate the obsessiveness of the characters.

Molière's use of farce indicates that the play is less apparently sophisticated than has generally been supposed. It also confirms that the dramatist had not turned his back on the genre which had brought him initial success. Right to the end of his career, he continued the experiment begun with *Les Précieuses ridicules,* which was quite revolutionary at the time: 'faire rire les honnêtes gens', that is, getting audiences to laugh at comedy, and not merely at farce. His handling of farcical material in *Les Femmes savantes* is subtle and complex, and his play is far superior to its sources in the Farce. The secret lay in Molière's ability to integrate the different genres into a coherent whole. The means by which he has achieved this unity will be examined in my next chapter.

[19] 'LE DOCTEUR: Sais-tu bien d'où vient le mot de galant homme? LE BARBOUILLÉ. Qu'il vienne de Villejuif, ou d'Aubervilliers, je ne m'en soucie guère.'

7

Coherence

T H E organic unity of the play has been frequently disputed. In the seventeenth century, and in particular from 1640 onwards, attention was increasingly given to order and harmony. One of the characteristics of the great plays of Molière's time was their aesthetic coherence. I shall assess the play in the light of the period's exigencies of unity, firstly the unities of time, place and action.

UNITY OF TIME

The unity of time (all events should take place within twenty-four hours) presents few problems. Past action is minimal and is referred to in conversations: Clitandre's two-year courtship of Armande and the transfer of his affection to Henriette; Trissotin's foppish behaviour; Chrysale's womanizing in Italy in his youth. Philaminte's bringing forward of the wedding ('dès ce soir') ensures that the action will be completed within 'one revolution of the sun'. The afternoon and early evening sessions prove rather hectic, with the dismissal and reinstatement of the maid, the reading party, the comings and goings of Ariste and Chrysale, Vadius's delivery of books, and the signing of the contract. However, Molière is not primarily concerned with exact representation of everyday reality, with what post-nineteenth century critics might call 'realism'. Events are telescoped for dramatic effect, to create tension (particularly for the characters, who await the outcome of the marriage interest). The unity of time is subjected to imaginative selection of the most important happenings.

UNITY OF PLACE

Study of the function of place and setting has been largely neglected, partly on account of the lack of contemporary evidence (there are no indications of Molière's *mise-en-scène* and the *décorateur* Mahelot's record cites only the most obvious props: 'Le théâtre est une chambre; il faut deux livres, quatre chaises et du papier'), partly on account of the unfavourable comparison between décor in tragedy and comedy.[20] Although the setting for *Les Femmes savantes* is not as evocative as for example the altar, the temple, the palace or the seraglio in the plays of Racine, it nevertheless contributes to the play's unity and comic interest.

The play's unified setting matches that of Molière's two greatest creations, *Le Misanthrope* and *Tartuffe*.[21] The street, the *carrefour* or the public square – the typical locus in Molière's early plays – have been replaced by a single room in Chrysale's house. Extraneous comedy from outdoor settings – abductions, serenades, nocturnal escapes, chance encounters with passers-by ('funny things happen on the way to the forum') – gives way to a more carefully integrated comic structure, focusing on the life of the family. Comic symbolism is expressed in the setting and in the props mentioned by the characters. The clash between old and new is represented by the plethora of new-fangled scientific gadgets which Chrysale describes as 'cent brimborions' and the conventional signs of bourgeois wealth like 'miroir' and 'porcelaine', and no doubt rather unfashionable Louis XIII furniture. The vast library ('livres éternels') clashes with the bourgeois interior (Philaminte has probably chosen the books for size to impress visitors – Chrysale would retain one for weight, to press his collars!). Philaminte's drawing-room is a far cry from its

[20] An interesting attempt to correct the imbalance has been made by Q. Hope, 'Place and setting in *Tartuffe*', *PMLA*, 89 (1974), 42-49.

[21] 'The dominant fact about the setting is that for only the third time, and the last, in his career, Molière situated the action of a full-length play in a single interior' (R. W. Herzel, 'The *Décor* of Molière's Stage: The Testimony of Brissart and Chauveau', *PMLA*, 93 [1978], p. 950). However, Herzel finds the unity of décor constricting.

model, the aristocratic salon, which would have been decor-
ated and furnished to a uniformly exquisite taste. The bluestockings' attempt to turn their lounge into a high-class salon
is as ludicrous as their efforts to build an observatory in the
attic (a room not visible to the audience).

The setting further degrades the use of heroic language in
the play. The power struggle between Chrysale and Philaminte and the battle for literary supremacy between the male
pedants are waged in a bourgeois drawing room and not on
any illustrious field of battle. Although grounded in an
identifiable social reality, the setting illustrates the fantasy
element of the play. The four main characters who live
outside, Trissotin, Clitandre, Vadius and Ariste, bring an
external reality to bear on the bourgeois household. But in
the case of Trissotin and Vadius, their reality is as extrava-
gant as that of Chrysale and the female pedants. The four
outsiders are contrasted in pairs: Clitandre and Trissotin;
Vadius and Ariste. Ironically, Trissotin is attracted to the
household by the very objects which Philaminte disdains but
which Chrysale prizes; Clitandre's sole interest is in Henriette. Vadius sees in the home an opportunity to read his
work, whereas Ariste, as a member of the family, has a
specific interest in promoting the marriage between Clitandre
and Henriette ('Savez-vous ce qui m'amène ici? [...] Mais
venons au sujet qui m'amène en ces lieux', 334, 350). Both
Vadius and Ariste seek to disabuse the bluestockings of
Trissotin by exposing the sonneteer's fortune-hunting. Vadius's letter fails because it is self-centred and because he
believes the ladies are truly interested in literary merit and
therefore the question of plagiarism; Ariste's letters succeed
because of his detachment and because he perceives that the
ladies' fantasy is impenetrable and consequently that he
needs to appeal to Trissotin's self-interest and greed. With
few outsiders, entrances and exits are plausibly motivated.
Characters frequently appear when discussed (e.g. I, 1-2; I,
3-4; IV, 4-5; V, 2-3). Expressions like 'Je l'aperçois qui vient'
(119) or 'Mais je vois votre tante' (270) are a traditional
means of introducing new characters in comedy. They allow
Molière to respect the *liaison de scènes,* a convention not

observed as strictly in seventeenth-century comedy as in
tragedy (see for example the cruder scene joinery of some of
Molière's early works).

UNITY OF ACTION

Events are not casually strung together, but, as we have
seen in chapters 1 and 2, the plot is quite tightly constructed.
The first two acts reveal abortive attempts by Clitandre and
Chrysale to promote the marriage between the lovers: Clitandre's attempts founder on the hostility of Armande and on
the folly of Bélise, Chrysale's on his own pusillanimity and
on the intransigence of Philaminte. In the middle, the third
act, the balance is finely held, with first the *femmes savantes'*
group, then the conservatives holding the ascendancy. The
occupation of the stage symbolizes the conflict: one represen-
tative of the conservatives, Henriette, sits in on the first four
scenes, then Armande remains behind in the last two scenes
when the conservatives take over. In III, 2 – the centre of the
play by virtue 'of its actual position – the action 'reaches a
plateau'. The sonnet scene is not as digressive as has been
supposed. It shows the marked contrast between the 'displaced sexuality' of the bluestockings and the natural love
between Clitandre and Henriette. From III, 3 onwards, the
balance tilts in favour of the lovers, though not without
moments of tension for them and their supporters, as we have
seen in chapter 1. Acts IV and V invert Acts I and II. The
departure of Vadius (III, 3) and his denunciation of Trissotin
(IV, 4) and the return of Martine (V, 2) reverse the losses
sustained in the first two acts, and anticipate the denouement.

The creation of three roles – Bélise, Martine and Vadius –
is thought to have introduced three sub-plots which are more
or less 'self-contained and not strictly necessary to the action
of the play'. It has been suggested that Martine and Bélise
were added as an afterthought on account of changes which
took place in Molière's pool of actors between 1670 (when
the play was being composed) and 1672 (when it was produ-

ced).[22] All three roles can be justified on dramaturgical grounds. Bélise has a triple function: she offers a false obstacle to the lovers, represents the extreme view of Armande's pseudo-metaphysical attitude to love, and caricatures the *savante* aspirations of Philaminte and Armande. Martine's role is less important than that of the servants in other plays by Molière, in which the lovers are less fully developed. However, she does act as an indirect support in her encouragement of the weak-willed Chrysale. Her introduction in II, 5 is not gratuitous but follows the pattern of *Le Misanthrope* and *Tartuffe* in which the symptoms of a problem are presented before the problem itself. In *Le Misanthrope,* the question of sincerity is broached before Alceste's relationship with Célimène; in *Tartuffe,* hypocrisy and false devotion are mentioned before the Tartuffe-Mariane-Valère triangle; in *Les Femmes savantes,* the pedantry of Philaminte is shown before her opposition to the lovers. The two aspects are interdependent. Vadius's role amplifies the part of Trissotin, and balances that of the maid. His letter unleashes the *coup de théâtre* of the marriage announcement, and advances the denouement.

Perhaps the most compelling argument for the inclusion of the three roles is their contribution to the equilibrium of the play. To update Brisson's sporting imagery, the play could be considered a game of five-a-side (if one excludes the minor roles): father, celibate uncle, daughter, suitor, maid versus mother, maiden aunt, daughter, rival lover, pedant. The verbal symmetry is almost perfect with 50 % of the lines being delivered by Chrysale's side and 49 % by Philaminte's (see *40,* pp. 51-52). The equal distribution contributes to the dramatic interest (a football match between Brazil and the Isle of Man would hardly be an absorbing spectacle!).

A statistical analysis of the number of speeches by each character confirms the overall balance and shows the distorted emphasis of modern productions which have focused on

---

[22] See Herzel, *44,* p. 227. For a refutation of his theory see J. F. Gaines, 'Commentary on Roger Herzel's "Problems in the Original Casting"', ibid., pp. 241-48.

one or two characters: 'of the total 1778 lines, Philaminte speaks 283 (16 %), Clitandre 273 (15 %), Henriette 236 (13 %), Chrysale 233 (13 %), Armande 217 (12 %), Trissotin 181 (10 %), Bélise 140 (8 %), Ariste 97 (5 %), Vadius 53 (3 %) and Martine 47 (3 %)' (see *46*, p. 154, n. 18; *6*, pp. 31-32).

THE DENOUEMENT

The ending, like so many in Molière's theatre, has been considered illogical and highly improbable. Molière's contemporaries were very satisfied with it: the device of the forged letters, says its first reviewer, 'n'est pas une moins belle invention que l'Exempt dans *L'Imposteur* [*Tartuffe*]'. In fact, it is arguably very much better. The denouement is constructed around yet another comic paradox, the use of artifice to expose reality. Ariste's false news unmasks Trissotin and reveals the genuineness of Clitandre. The ending is very carefully prepared and comes from within the play. No character is suddenly introduced to bring about the final reversal: the denouement is the culmination of the plot. Ariste, who has been presented as a 'sage personne', has protested throughout his intention to help the lovers. The audience anticipates some artifice from his final remark in Act IV: 'J'emploierai toute chose à servir vos amours' (1448).

Objections have been levelled at Trissotin's prompt capitulation. Trissotin has however become careless, having got away with much more than he could have thought possible. After Philaminte's total disregard of Vadius's allegations, he clearly (on the basis of his confidence in V, 1) entertains delusions of infallibility. Furthermore, the financial collapse is not implausible. The attributed cause of the loss of Philaminte's lawsuit ('la grande négligence que vous avez pour vos affaires' and 'Le peu de soin que vous avez [...]') is perfectly in keeping with the latter's indifference to everyday matters. Chrysale's accommodating temperament, imperceptiveness, and willingness to delegate the management of his affairs to others make his bankruptcy quite credible.

The lack of coherence of the characters in the denouement has also been widely criticized. Normally, there are no
conversions in Molière's plays. This play, however, has been
regarded as an exception, and scholars have found the ending
to be distinctly optimistic. Admittedly, the happy marriage
and the exclusion of the villain convey a state of general
well-being. But the restoration of order is not permanent:
there is no reason to suppose that there will be any lasting
reconciliation in the Chrysale household. There is a sufficient
change in the situation for a limited reconciliation so that the
plot can be resolved. The last obstacle to the lovers' happiness, Philaminte's opposition, has been removed. But the
problems of the main characters are unsolved.

The salient features of each character are expressed in
their final lines. Philaminte's confession of her error has led
many to believe that she has seen the light. It is true that
Molière does not generally blacken his monomaniacs com-
pletely, but shows that, monomania apart, they may have
admirable human traits (which sharpen the attack on monomania) – witness here Philaminte's disinterestedness with regard to the loss of her wealth, and her belief (albeit naive) that
others are like her. In this respect the ending is somewhat
curious as far as her characterization is concerned: she is less
of a comic butt than elsewhere, and saves what can be saved
of the situation. However, the ending reveals that she is not
cured of her monomania. If she remains true to herself, it is
ambiguously: note her comically obsessive linguistic criticism; her assertiveness, even in the change of direction – she
is still very much in control of the house and will continue to
get her own way. She has learned her lesson as far as
Trissotin is concerned, intellectually, but not emotionally –
like so many of Molière's comic heroes! There will be other
Trissotins! She fails to perceive the vanity of her pretensions – her pedantry, her academic affectation, and her ap-
palling literary taste – which made her an easy target for the
likes of Trissotin. She addresses no word of apology to
Henriette, whom she has so misused, and, in fact, in her final
speech redirects her insensitivity towards her own sex to
Armande. Philaminte's stoicism is, we have seen, contradict-

ed by her frequent loss of control elsewhere and at the end by her pleasure in Trissotin's punishment (she needs a scapegoat). It is also surpassed by the generosity shown by both Clitandre and Henriette.

Armande's final line confirms my interpretation of Molière's ironic presentation of the role. The plaintive, self-pitying appeal to her mother contrasts with her vigorous, aggressive, exclamatory opening lines. Armande's reliance on 'philosophie' is exposed as sham. Like her mother, she fails to accept responsibility for the situation – the loss of Clitandre is self-inflicted. The only measure of enlightenment is evident in Armande's silence, which probably signifies her breaking away from her mother's domination.

Bélise's curtain line shows that she is still locked up in her fantasy world, and that she has, if anything, become theatrically certifiable. Still convinced that Clitandre loves her, she warns him that he may regret marrying someone else out of desperation. There is an element of unconscious irony in the old maid's riddle: Clitandre's marriage to Henriette has, on his own admission, been contracted out of desperation at waiting for Armande. Trissotin's hypocrisy is reflected in his justification of his withdrawal on grounds of family opposition and his own qualms over an enforced marriage – problems which have not troubled him until Ariste's disclosures (note the contrast between his words in V, 1 and V, 4). Chrysale's materialistic interests are expressed in his reactions to the reported loss of the family money: 'Votre procès perdu! [...] O Ciel! tout à la fois perdre ainsi tout mon bien!' His triumphal boast which closes the play shows his verbal hubris:

> Je le savais bien, moi, que vous l'épouseriez [...]
> Allons, monsieur, suivez l'ordre que j'ai prescrit,
> Et faites le contrat ainsi que je l'ai dit.

He claims the principal part in the happy ending, but the audience knows that he has been a mere spectator. Ariste's final speech serves to explain the trick to Henriette in order to remove her last-minute reservations about the marriage. It confirms his role as the chief ally of the lovers.

The lovers say nothing after 1758. In their final speeches both offer a counterpoint to the characters with whom they have been contrasted: Henriette's practical awareness of the effect of money on love reflects her realism in the opening scene, and her sacrificial gesture contrasts with Armande's mock-sacrificial plaint; Clitandre's genuineness and generosity emphasize Trissotin's falsehood and self-interest.

The plot and ideas are closely integrated. One of the reasons for this is that the plot, which revolves around the marriage, is also one of the main themes. In addition, the discursive scenes show the warped mental processes which lie behind the opposition to the marriage. The *femmes savantes* theme is also related to the power struggle in the home, in which Henriette is used as a pawn by both Chrysale and Philaminte. The dramatic parallelism conveyed by the even distribution of roles is reflected in the binary opposition between 'âme' and 'corps', 'matière', and 'sens', 'chair' and 'esprit' (see *48*).

Linguistic coherence is served by the use of recurrent imagery, especially metaphors drawn from the spheres of food, animals, books and sewing. The repeated use of antitheses, the most dominant linguistic feature, gives cogency to the disparate views and reinforces the comic and dramatic parallelism seen elsewhere.

8

'Une pièce tout-à-fait achevée'

In the preceding chapters I have tried to examine Molière's comic and dramatic artistry in the play. The cool reception given by some modern critics is largely unjustified. To dismiss the work as sexist and bourgeois is to ignore the perspective of the play, and, paradoxically, to adopt the uncritical attitude of the bluestockings. Male possessiveness is caricatured as much as female tyranny. Ignorance and pedantry serve as opposite poles of the dramatic spectrum.

The social element is admittedly rather dated. The satirical element, too, is only of historical interest today. But Molière uses a recognizable social setting in which he can situate comic types: these have not lost their appeal three hundred years on. The *femmes savantes* have not disappeared, even in our post-feminist society! In both academic and non-academic circles, pedants are to be found of both sexes, parading their knowledge for their own advancement; sometimes they dress up their propositions in high-sounding moral principles; they espouse all the latest jargon for the authority they think it will give them, ironically moving further and further away from the rational norm they claim to represent; nominalists, they indiscriminately apply their labels to whatever they read – or write about; they regard themselves as crypto-metalinguists, post-neo-transcendental-deconstructionalists, *et quoi d'autre encore* (what fun Molière would have made of all the '-ists'!); clear-sighted with regard to the failings of others, but myopic with regard to their own, they do not recognize their portraits, however accurately drawn. Trissotin, too, is still around! His methodology is unchanged but his interest in poetry (no longer in vogue) has given way to any fashionable disguise which will bring in

money! The modern Vadius is always seeking someone to
whom he can show his work, and will use all types of flattery
to win a sympathetic audience. The hen-pecked Chrysale,
whose authority is only in his imagination, is still capable of
provoking laughter in our post-patriarchal society. *Les
Femmes savantes* puts us on guard against vanity, self-
interest and pretentiousness, in all its manifestations, and
invites us to think about the gap in our own lives between
illusion and reality.

To what extent did Molière achieve his reputed aim:
'une pièce tout-à-fait achevée'? We shall never know whether
he felt satisfied with the work on which he seems to have
spent so much time. Various theories have been advanced to
explain the delay between the play's original conception and
its first performance. The most satisfactory explanation, to
my mind, is not circumstantial but aesthetic. Molière was
seeking in the last play in which there was no musical
collaboration to attain the perfect form. He has left us an
'exhibition piece', an 'anthology of his capabilities', a testimony to his theatrical craftsmanship. Viewed in this light, the
play ranks as one of his masterpieces.

Bibliography

IN view of the vast amount of critical material on Molière's work, the selection given below cannot be comprehensive. The studies included are those I have found to be most useful to an appreciation of *Les Femmes savantes*. Many take a very different view of the play from the one I have put forward.

ŒUVRES COMPLÈTES

1. *Œuvres complètes* (Les Grands Ecrivains de la France), ed. E. Despois et P. Mesnard, Paris, Hachette, 1873-1900, 13 vols. (The authoritative edition, with very useful critical material, particularly in the notes.)
2. *Œuvres complètes* (Bibl. de la Pléiade), ed. G. Couton, Paris, Gallimard, 1971, 2 vols.

SEPARATE EDITIONS

3. *Les Femmes savantes* (Classiques France), ed. P. Mélèse, Paris, Hachette, 1948.
4. *Les Femmes savantes* (special number of *L'Avant-scène*, no. 409-10, pp. 1-71), Paris, 1968. (Useful for production guide.)
5. *Les Femmes savantes* (Les Classiques du peuple), ed. J. Cazalbou et Denise Sévely, Paris, Editions Sociales, 1971.
6. *Les Femmes savantes* (Clarendon French Series), ed. H. G. Hall, O. U. P., 1974.

GENERAL AND BACKGROUND STUDIES

7. Adam, A., *Histoire de la littérature française au XVIIᵉ siècle*, Paris, Domat, 1952, 5 vols (particularly vol. III).
8. Bénichou, P., *Morales du Grand Siècle*, Paris, Gallimard, 1948.
9. Bergson, H., *Le Rire. Essai sur la signification du comique*, Paris, F. Alcan, 1900.
10. Bray, R., *Molière, homme de théâtre*, Paris, Mercure de France, 1954.

11. Brereton, G., *French Comic Drama from the Sixteenth to the Eighteenth Century,* London, Methuen, 1977.
12. Collinet, J.-P., *Lectures de Molière,* Paris, Colin, 1974.
13. Conesa, G., *Le Dialogue moliéresque: étude stylistique et dramaturgique,* Paris, P. U. F., 1983.
14. Descotes, M., *Les Grands Rôles du théâtre de Molière,* Paris, P. U. F., 1960.
15. Eustis, A., *Molière as Ironic Contemplator,* The Hague-Paris, Mouton, 1973.
16. Fernandez, R., *La Vie de Molière,* Paris, Gallimard, 1929.
17. Garapon, R., *Le Dernier Molière,* Paris, CDU-SEDES, 1977.
18. Grene, N., *Shakespeare, Jonson, Molière: The Comic Contract,* London, Macmillan, 1980.
19. Gutwirth, M., *Molière ou l'invention comique,* Paris, Minard, 1966.
20. Hall, H. G., *Comedy in Context. Essays on Molière,* Jackson, University of Mississippi Press, 1984.
21. Howarth, W. D., (ed.) *Comic Drama. The European Heritage,* London, Methuen, 1978.
22. ———, *Molière. A Playwright and his Audience,* C. U. P., 1982.
23. Hubert, J. D., *Molière and the Comedy of Intellect,* Berkeley, California University Press, 1962.
24. Jouvet, L., *Molière et la comédie classique (extraits des cours de Louis Jouvet au Conservatoire 1939-40),* Paris, Gallimard, 1965.
25. Knutson, H. C., *Molière: An Archetypal Approach,* Toronto, University of Toronto Press, 1976.
26. Lawrence, F. L., *Molière: The Comedy of Unreason,* New Orleans, Tulane University, 1968.
27. McBride, R., *The Sceptical Vision of Molière. A Study in Paradox,* London, Macmillan, 1977.
28. Moore, W. G., *Molière. A New Criticism,* Oxford, Clarendon Press, 1949.
29. Reynier, G., *La Femme au XVIIᵉ siècle,* Paris, Tallandier, 1929.
30. Scherer, J., *La Dramaturgie classique en France,* Paris, Nizet, 1950.

STUDIES OF 'LES FEMMES SAVANTES'

31. Arnavon, J., *La Mise-en-scène des 'Femmes savantes' de Molière,* Paris, Desfosses, 1912.
32. Reynier, G., *'Les Femmes savantes' de Molière,* Paris, Mellottée, 1936.
33. Chevalley, Sylvie, *Les Femmes savantes – Monographie,* Paris, Comédie-Française, 1962. (Collection of studies by Sylvie Chevalley, P. Mélèse, G. Reynier, and J. Truchet.)
34. Wilbur, R., *The Learned Ladies,* New York, Harcourt, 1978. (A translation with a useful introduction.)
35. Gaillard, P., *'Les Précieuses ridicules' / 'Les Femmes savantes' de Molière,* Paris, Hatier (Profil d'une œuvre, 66), 1979.

ARTICLES

36. Barnwell, H. T., 'Molière's Language and the Expectation of Comedy', *Studi francesi*, 19 (1975), 34-47.

37. Bratto, O., 'Molière, *Les Femmes savantes*, études d'anthroponymie littéraire', *Revue internationale d'onomastique*, XXV (1973), 257-69.

38. Brooks, W., 'Has Trissotin been misjudged?', *Modern Languages*, LXVI (1985), 27-36.

39. Eustis, A., 'The Nature of Molière's Satire', *Romance Notes*, XV (1973-74), Suppl. 1, 5-14.

40. Gaines, J. F., 'Ménage versus Salon in *Les Femmes savantes*', *Esprit créateur*, XXI, 3 (Fall, 1981), 51-59.

41. Gossen, Jr, E. J., '*Les Femmes savantes*. Métaphore et mouvement dramatique', *The French Review*, XLV (1971-72), 37-45.

42. Gutwirth, M., 'Molière and the Woman Question: *Les Précieuses ridicules, L'Ecole des femmes, Les Femmes savantes*', *Theatre Journal*, 34 (1982), 345-59.

43. Henning, G. N., 'The Dénouement of *Les Femmes savantes*', *The French Review*, XIII (1939-40), 42-45.

44. Herzel, R. W., 'Problems in the Original Casting of *Les Femmes savantes*', *Actes de New Orleans*, (Biblio 17[5]) Tübingen, *PFSCL* (1982), 215-31.

45. Hope, Q., 'Animals in Molière', *PMLA*, 79 (1964), 411-21.

46. Howarth, W. D., '*Une pièce tout-à-fait achevée*: Aesthetic Coherence in *Les Femmes savantes*' in *Form and Meaning: Aesthetic Coherence in Seventeenth-Century French Drama*, ed. W. D. Howarth, I. McFarlane, Margaret McGowan, Amersham, Avebury, 1982, 142-55.

47. Jeune, S., 'Molière, le pédant et le pouvoir: note pour le commentaire des *Femmes savantes*', *RHLF*, 55 (1955), 145-54.

48. Molino, J., 'Les Nœuds de la matière: l'unité des *Femmes savantes*', *XVIIᵉ siècle*, 113 (1976), 23-47.

49. Mourgues, Odette de, 'Molière et le comique de la préciosité' in *Mélanges offerts à Georges Couton*, Lyon, Presses Universitaires de Lyon, 1981, 403-12.

50. Périvier, J.-H., 'Equivoques moliéresques. Le sonnet de Trissotin', *RSH*, XXXVIII (1973), 543-54.

51. Rey-Debove, Josette, 'L'Orgie langagière. Le sonnet à la princesse Uranie', *Poétique*, III (1972), 572-83.

52. Shaw, D., '*Les Femmes savantes* and Feminism', *Journal of European Studies*, 14 (1984), 24-38.

53. Suther, Judith D., 'The Tricentennial of Molière's *Femmes savantes*', *The French Review*, XLV (Special Issue, 4, 1972), 31-38.

54. Truchet, J., 'Molière et *Les Femmes savantes*' in *Onze études sur l'image de la femme dans la littérature française du dix-septième siècle*, Paris, Jean-Michel Place, 1978, 91-101.

55. Wilson, J. C., 'Expansion and Brevity in Molière's Style', in *Molière: Stage and Study. Essays in Honour of W. G. Moore*, ed. W. D. Howarth and M. Thomas, O. U. P., 1973, 93-113.

CRITICAL GUIDES TO FRENCH TEXTS

edited by
Roger Little, Wolfgang van Emden, David Williams